WHEN GOD SAYS
YES

PRAYER AND THE WILL OF GOD

Dwayne E. Mercer

ISBN: 978-0-615-55044-2
LCCN: 2011918223

Printed by Gorham Printing, Centralia, Washington USA

*This book is dedicated to my wife, Pam,
who is my greatest answer to prayer.*

ACKNOWLEDGEMENTS

A special word of thanks to all of you who helped make this book possible and to those whose stories I've shared here.

CONTENTS

INTRODUCTION

W hy write another book on prayer? Because even though there are over 5,000 books already available on the subject, people still struggle with getting answers in their prayer lives.[1] 91 percent of women and 85 percent of men in America say they pray regularly, but only 15 percent of them feel that they receive consistent answers to their prayers.[2]

I believe one of the major reasons for atheism is a lack of answered prayer. The Bible says, *"God has set eternity in our hearts."* Romans teaches that God has placed the knowledge of Himself in the hearts of people. Yet, many as they get older turn away from God. Many who were raised in church have dropped out. Some are angry with God; others are ambivalent.

I have spoken to many atheists, agnostics and general church drop-outs during my years of ministry. The source of their doubt and disobedience often stemmed from a crisis experience in their lives. They prayed that God would not allow their parents to divorce—but they divorced. They prayed for their sister to live— but she died. The one time in their lives they felt they had a crucial need that only God could meet, they prayed—but there was no answer. They felt hurt by God and a cycle of unbelief, anger and disillusionment began in their hearts. Ravi Zacharias wrote in his book, *Has Christianity Failed You?*

> I sat with a man in my car, talking about a series of heartbreaks he had experienced. "There were just a few things I had wanted in life, he said. None of them have turned out the way I had prayed. I wanted my parents to live until I was at least able to stand on my own and they could watch my children grow up. It didn't happen. I wanted my marriage to succeed, and it didn't. I wanted my children to grow up grateful for what God had given them. That didn't happen. I wanted my business to prosper, and it didn't. Not only have my prayers amounted to nothing; the exact opposite has happened. Don't even ask me if you can pray for me. I am left with no trust of any kind in such things."
>
> I felt two emotions rising up within me as I listened. The first was one of genuine sorrow. He felt that he had tried, that he had done his part, but that God hadn't lived up to His end of the deal. The second emotion was one of helplessness, as I wondered where to begin trying to help him.[3]

What would you say to this man? At some point in your life you may have felt the same way. Sometimes it's not that people do not believe in God, but rather they are hurt and believe God is the author of that hurt. They think that if God truly does exist, He does not care about them or else He would have answered their prayers.

This book was written to help you better understand how prayer works. When we pray, there are three possible answers— yes, no, or wait. When does God say *yes?* How can you get more yes answers to your prayers?

This book begins with a chapter on the mystery of prayer and is followed by five chapters concerning the essentials of prayer, which are: dependence, direction, devotion, desire and determination. The final chapter will attempt to answer the question, "Why do we need more *yes* answers to our prayers?" In this second edition I have added an appendage on prayer and fasting.

As you read this book, I hope that you will do so with a hunger in your heart. If you can better understand the theology of prayer, you can better understand God. If you have a better understanding of God, you can trust Him on a deeper level and, therefore, follow Him in a more intentional way. As you will discover, the closer you follow, the more *yes* answers you will receive to your prayers.

THE MYSTERY OF
ANSWERED PRAYER

CHAPTER 1

THE MYSTERY OF
ANSWERED PRAYER

Prayer is as mysterious as it is frustrating. When was the last time you had a definite answer to prayer? Do you believe when you pray that God is going to answer your prayer?

I once saw the now deceased comedian, George Carlin, on a television show. He defiantly proclaimed that he did not believe in God. When asked who he prayed to, he replied, (actor) "Joe Pesci." As the audience laughed, he was asked what the results were. He replied, "Oh, about fifty-fifty. Same as when you Christians pray to God." Well, I know many Christians who would gladly take the fifty-fifty.

Whether it's a parent praying for their rebellious teenager, a wife praying for her marriage, or a man praying about a job, I have heard the frustration hundreds of times—"What's the use? God never hears my prayer."

As a little girl jumped into bed, her dad asked her, "Honey, did you say your prayers?" "No" she replied. "I didn't say them tonight." "Why not?" asked the dad. "Well, I figured that God maybe got tired of hearing the same old prayer, so I read Him the story of Little Red Riding Hood."

Some believers want the Lord to come out of a genie's bottle and give them what they feel they need; for others, how they feel about God is determined by how God "performs" in their prayer life. However, most of us just want to know that God is intimately involved in our lives. We want to be special to Him—to feel loved. When we consistently find our prayers going unanswered, we are tempted to think that perhaps God doesn't care. We become frustrated with God and question His promises.

One of those promises is found in the book of Jeremiah. *"Call to Me and I will answer you, and I will tell you great and mighty things, which you do not know." (Jeremiah 33:3)* In this verse, we are given a glimpse of the answer to the mystery of prayer.

THE BACKGROUND

Jeremiah is called the weeping prophet. He lamented over the sins of Judah. In the Bible, we discover that in 930 BC the kingdom of Israel was divided over some bad decisions made by David's grandson, King Rehoboam. The ten tribes of the north kept the name Israel and two tribes to the south took the name Judah. Because of sin and their departure from God, Israel had been captured by Assyria in 722 BC.[1] Now over 150 years later, Judah was traveling down the same path of disobedience. Jeremiah was placed in jail for calling the nation to repentance. While Jeremiah was in prison, God made a great prayer promise to him.

There are three distinct parts to the promise: the request, God's response and the results.

THE REQUEST

The word "call" in the original Hebrew language is an imperative or command. Literally, we are to *cry* out to God.[2] Why cry out to God if He already knows what you are going to ask, if He already knows what the answer will be? God is all knowing; He is sovereign—so what's the point?

First, realize that prayer is a means of communication with God. There are two primary ways that God communicates: through prayer and through the Bible. Communication is the vital ingredient that links relationships together. Whether it's a relationship between husband and wife, parent and child, or a friendship—there is little quality in the relationship without communication.

In order to get heart-to-heart with God, there must be active communication. Charles Spurgeon said,

> "The very act of prayer is a blessing. To pray is, as it were, to bathe oneself in a cool stream, and so to escape from the heat of earth's summer sun. To pray is to mount on eagle's wings above the clouds and soar to heaven where God dwells. To pray is to enter the treasure house of God and to enrich oneself out of an inexhaustible storehouse. To pray is to grasp heaven in one's arms; to embrace the deity within one's soul and to feel one's body made a temple of the Holy Ghost."[3]

Dr. Charles Stanley said, *"The greatest thing about prayer is a feeling of oneness with God."*[4]

Think about it. Through Christ we are able to get in touch with the God who created the universe. Before Jesus died on the cross, the veil in the temple separated the Holy Place in the temple from the Holy of Holies. This special place housed the Ark of the

Covenant, which represented the presence of God in the nation of Israel. Only the High Priest, once a year, was allowed beyond the veil. The High Priest would sprinkle the blood of a goat for the forgiveness of Israel's sins for the coming year. It was an awesome event. It was also a horrifying event. If anyone touched the Ark of the Covenant, they would immediately die. The veil represented man's separation from God.

When Christ died on the cross, the veil was torn in half by the very hand of God. *"And behold, the veil of the temple was torn in two from top to bottom; and the earth shook and the rocks were split." (Matthew 27:51)* Now we have access to God 24/7. Those who have come to Christ for salvation can now come to God at anytime, and any place, to pray. We are given the opportunity to have an active relationship with God. Think about it—you have a greater access to God than even the prophets of the Old Testament.

There is a second reason why we need to pray. There are times if we do not pray, God will not give us what He desires us to have. *"...You do not have because you do not ask." (James 4:2)*

I like to think of God's will for our lives as *the path of blessing*. When we are on the path of blessing, God has gifts waiting for us. If we are off this path, we are going to miss out on many of His blessings. Imagine with me for a moment. You are walking down life's path and God blesses you with what you need in order to continue to follow Him. He gives you these things even when you do not ask. After all, how many of us pray for good health every day or for traveling mercies to and from work? The simple things in life often go unnoticed because God blesses us without our asking.

There are many other times, however, as we travel down this road that God has special gifts waiting for us that we do not receive because we do not ask. The gift could be that special person, that great job, a financial windfall, healing, or a witnessing opportunity. I believe that when we get to heaven, we will discover that there were a multitude of things we could have had, but we missed out on them because we did not ask.

WHY, THEN, DON'T WE PRAY?

First, God blesses us whether we pray or not. Since we are blessed, we often fail to see our deepest needs. We subconsciously reason, "God is going to give me what I need, so why ask?" We become presumptuous with God. It's amazing when we think that the gifts from God actually keep us from receiving great and mighty things.

The second reason we do not pray more is a lack of humility. Prayer is really an unnatural act. We all tend to be self-sufficient. I am guilty of this myself. Prayer, in a sense, is an assault on the human autonomy. We must realize that self-sufficiency is reserved for God alone. Although it's not listed in any book on the attributes of God, it nevertheless could be categorized as one. We do not try to claim the other attributes of God. As a believer, I recognize that I am not all-powerful, all-knowing, everywhere at once, all-loving, or ruler over the universe. So, why do I think I can be self-sufficient? **If you want a barometer for humility, it can be measured by this question: How much do you pray?** Every time you pray you say to God, "Lord, I can't do it alone. I must share with you my deepest desires and ask for your help."

A third reason we fail to pray is spiritual warfare. If you are not aware of the intense spiritual warfare that takes place during prayer, let me suggest a simple exercise. Try to pray silently for five minutes and see how your mind wanders. Look at the example of

Daniel when he prayed for three weeks (Daniel 10:10-17). An angel tried to send Daniel his answer immediately, but the Prince of the kingdom of Persia (a demon) fought him. Satan keeps you from praying. He gets your mind off prayer when you are on your knees and he discourages you when the answer is delayed.

A fourth and primary reason we do not pray enough is because we do not feel we receive enough answers.

GOD'S RESPONSE

Jeremiah 33:3 says, *"Call to me and I will answer you..."*

It helps us to realize as we call that we are praying to God. We do not pray to an angel, a saint or a limited deity, but have access to the throne of the almighty, all powerful God of the universe. R. A. Torrey said,

> "We must have a definite and vivid realization that God is bending over us, and listening as we pray. In very much of our prayer, there is really but little thought of God. Our mind is taken up with the thought of what we need. It is not occupied with the thought of the mighty and loving Father."[5]

As we pray to God, we realize that prayer moves Him to action. There are three possible answers to our prayers—*yes, no,* and *wait.*

First, there is the *yes* answer. That is the answer we all want. We want to rub the genie's lamp and have the Lord appear to give us whatever we want. Although God is no genie, He does answer many prayers with a *yes.*

The second answer is *no.* No does not mean that we are in sin. If we are not believers or we are believers who have unconfessed sin, it's not that God will say no, but He will not acknowledge our prayer at all. I John 3:22 tells us *"...and whatever we ask we receive from Him, because we keep His commandments and do the things that are pleasing in His sight."*

Of course, God hears everything. When the Bible speaks of God not hearing a prayer, it means that although He technically hears, He is under no obligation to answer that prayer. If we are right with God, He will always answer. Sometimes the answer will be *no*. This means that God has something better. The late Ruth Graham (Billy Graham's wife) said that if God had answered all of her prayers (with a *yes* answer), she would have married the wrong man three different times!

We tend to think that if God says no, He just did not answer. Suppose a little boy asks his mom for ice cream before supper and she says no. He runs upstairs to his room, and his brother asks him, "What did you ask Mom?" "I asked her for ice cream," he replies. "What did she say?" asks the brother. "Oh, she didn't say anything" the boy says in disgust. God answers every prayer of a person in His path of blessing. Sometimes the answer is *yes* and sometimes *no*. *No* is nevertheless an answer.

Sometimes we ask and God waits to answer. Why? Perhaps He is bringing circumstances, people and places together in order for the prayer to be answered. Maybe there are others involved. There could be spiritual warfare or that He is trying to teach us something. It's similar to a parent-child relationship. It is dangerous for children to get everything they want, when they want it. James Dobson said, *"The worst thing you can do is not to give a child everything that he wants, but give him everything he wants— when he wants it. Waiting helps the child appreciate what he has."*[6] It's been said, "God's delays are not God's denials." All of us can think back on times when God's answers were delayed. In hindsight, we can understand why.

Of course, all of us want God to say *yes*. The good news is that if we are in God's path of blessing He always says something. God is intimately involved in our lives and He moves with wisdom and love.

THE RESULTS

Jeremiah 33:3 says *"Call to Me and I will answer you, and I will tell you great and mighty things, which you do not know."*

The Old Testament picture of great and mighty things is a fortress of walls. Walls around a city were its greatest defense and a massive, powerful army was needed to scale or tear down walls. God says that there are walls and barriers to knowledge and blessing. Deuteronomy 29:29 says, *"The secret things belong to the LORD our God, but the things revealed belong to us and to our sons forever..."*

You and I receive answers to prayer every day. God says *yes* to more requests than we realize. However, it's the great and mighty things that seem to be barriers to receiving knowledge, blessing and power that make us discouraged. It's a relative with cancer, the death of a loved one, the problematic marriage or the rebellious teenager that cause us to wonder and leave us frustrated.

For example, one of the most often voiced prayers is one for healing. Many have cooled in their affection for God because they felt God turned His back on them or a loved one when He had the power to heal. Does prayer make a real difference?

DOES PRAYER HEAL?

Dr. Larry Dawsey had forsaken the Lord and his faith during childhood. During residency, he encountered his first patient with terminal cancer. After hearing his limited options, the patient chose not to be treated. Dawsey observed that the patient was often visited by people of the church who prayed for him. A year later, the patient paid Dawsey a surprise visit, and he was completely free of cancer. The young doctor was truly amazed and began to do research. He found a study conducted in 1988 by Randall Byrd at San Francisco General Hospital that presented the most convincing argument. Nearly 400 patients in the coronary care unit were assigned either to a group that prayed daily with prayer groups or to another group that was not prayed for. The study was double-blind, therefore no one knew what group they were in. The "prayed for" groups were five times less likely to need antibiotics as well as two and one-half times less likely to develop congestive heart failure or suffer cardiac arrest. Had the study dealt with a new drug or surgical procedure instead of prayer, the results would have been hailed as a major breakthrough. [7]

My most dramatic answer to prayer came to me as a college student. When I was 18 years old, I was diagnosed with diabetes. I was blessed that they caught the disease early enough that I could treat it with diet. For four years I did pretty well keeping my sugar level under control. Then I began to cheat on my diet. When I was 22, my doctor told me I would have to begin taking insulin. Certainly this was bad news. Yet, I knew that I had been warned; I had no one to blame but myself. I asked God to forgive my lack of discipline and I accepted whatever the consequences were to come. I had a strange and wonderful peace about the situation.

I was due to go back to the doctor's office and take a three-hour test to determine the level of insulin that I would need. The night before the appointment, I prayed privately. I was not praying about my physical condition at the time, but just simply praying about things that God was laying upon my heart. As I was talking to God, He placed a burden on my heart that He did not want me to have diabetes. In response, I prayed that God would supernaturally heal me of the disease. I did not go to a faith healer, nor make a special deal with God—I simply asked.

I will never forget it. I knew from the moment I said "amen" that God had healed me. The next day I kept my appointment. After they drew blood for the test, I left to hang out at the Baptist Student Union building on the university campus. It never occurred to me that God had not performed a miracle and I was at total peace.

When I went back to the doctor's office and got ready to go in, the thought struck me, "What if I am not healed?" The momentary fear that struck my heart was not whether I would have to take shots everyday or perhaps die young; my fear was "If God did not heal me, what will this do to my faith?" I shook off the feeling of doubt and walked into the office. Immediately, my eyes met the nurse's as she was passing through the hall. I asked her how the test went. In disbelief, she replied, "You don't have it. I can't explain it, but your diabetes is gone." Since that day over 30 years ago, I have not had a moment's trouble with diabetes.

Over the years I have gone through times when I wondered if God really loved me and wanted to be involved in my life. Then I recall two things: first, the time I received Christ into my heart and second, the time that God healed me of a dreaded disease. God does great and mighty things.

God does answer prayer. There are three possible answers. The question is—how do you get God to say *yes*?

DEPENDENCE: TRUSTING IN GOD'S CHARACTER

CHAPTER 2

DEPENDENCE: TRUSTING IN GOD'S CHARACTER

Jesus said *"It shall be done to you according to your faith." (Matthew 9:29)*

"Therefore I say to you, all things for which you pray and ask, believe that you have received them, and they will be granted you." (Mark 11:24)

Here is the problem: On one hand, we cannot have great answers to prayer without believing God, on the other hand, we have a struggle believing God because we don't feel that He is answering our prayers. It reminds me of a recent experiment of cost and reward conducted with mice running through a maze. At the end of the maze was a trap door. The mouse had to run through the maze and push open the trap door to claim his reward—a piece of cheese. The mouse memorized the maze and became quite proficient in running through it and quickly claiming his prize. One day the experiment took a turn. As the mouse opened the trap door, he was sprayed in the face with cold water. The mouse was stunned, but he still wanted the cheese. The next day the mouse ran through the maze and was rewarded with cheese. One day he got the cheese;

the next day, water in the face. For several days this went on, alternating back and forth. The mouse had a nervous breakdown. He stopped going through the maze. He wanted the cheese, but not the cold water. He ended up just sitting in a corner. He could not make up his mind so he gave up.[1]

I think sometimes we feel like that mouse. Sometimes God says *yes* to our prayers; sometimes we feel slapped in the face with a *no*. We lose our confidence in prayer and often it becomes merely a last resort.

A few years ago, a lady spoke to me about her struggle with faith. She said that she would pray, but God would not answer her prayers because she did not have enough faith. As I questioned her, I asked, "Do you believe God loves you?" Her response was, "Yes." I then asked, "If you knew that your faith was not required to have God answer your prayers, do you believe God would answer them?" "Yes, absolutely," she responded. Her problem was that she had faith in God, but she was trying to have faith in her own faith.

Most of us can identify with this lady. We try to have faith in our faith. It's as if answers to prayer depend on us and how much faith we can muster, rather than trusting in an all-loving, almighty God. We believe God will do it, if only we believe strongly enough. Our prayer and faith become man-centered rather than God-centered.

In the gospel of Mark, Jesus addresses this matter of faith and its relationship to prayer. I said that when we pray there are three possible answers—*yes*, *no* and *wait*. Perhaps that sounds to you like *maybe yes* and *maybe no*, but it's important to realize that if you are a believer and are right with God, He will answer your prayers every time—sometimes *yes*, sometimes *no* and sometimes *wait*.

In fact, for some the problem is not a lack of faith, but a lack of patience. You have not waited long enough for the answer. This book, however, is about getting *yes* answers. This does require faith, but what kind of faith and faith in who or what? Scripture says,

"On the next day, when they had left Bethany, He became hungry. Seeing at a distance a fig tree in leaf, He went to see if perhaps He would find anything on it; and when He came to it, He found nothing but leaves, for it was not the season for figs. He said to it, "May no one ever eat fruit from you again!" And His disciples were listening. As they were passing by in the morning, they saw the fig tree withered from the roots up. Being reminded, Peter said to Him, "Rabbi, look, the fig tree which You cursed has withered." And Jesus answered saying to them, "Have faith in God. Truly I say to you, whoever says to this mountain, 'Be taken up and cast into the sea,' and does not doubt in his heart, but believes that what he says is going to happen, it will be granted him. Therefore I say to you, all things for which you pray and ask, believe that you have received them, and they will be granted you."
(Mark 11:12-14; 20-24)

In the first part of this story, Jesus and his disciples were leaving Jerusalem on their way to Bethany. Jesus became hungry and seeing a fig tree in the distance, He walked over to see if it bore any figs. He found nothing but leaves and pronounced a judgment on the tree. On their way back from Bethany, they came across the same fig tree and it was dead. When the disciples asked why the fig tree was dead, Jesus replied "Have faith in God." What was His point? To answer this question, we must first discover what He meant by faith.

A DESCRIPTION OF FAITH

Faith can be described as trusting in the honesty and character of another. The Bible gives a definitive description in the book of Hebrews.

> "Now faith is the assurance of things hoped for, the conviction of things not seen. For by it the men of old gained approval. By faith we understand that the worlds were prepared by the Word of God, so that what is seen was not made out of things which are visible." (Hebrews 11:1-3)

In this passage, we see that faith is described in three ways: the confidence of things hoped for, the conviction of things not seen and trusting the character of His Word.

First, it is confidence or assurance of things hoped for. Faith often has something to do with the future. There is a confident assurance in the promises of God. God has spoken and we believe strongly enough in His promise that it is as good as in our possession. A good example of this aspect of faith is our salvation. We know that because we trust Christ as our Savior and Lord, we will one day be in heaven. Although we are not in heaven yet, we still have an assurance or confidence in something in the future. Biblical hope is not wishful thinking, but complete trust in what God has for us in the future.

Second, faith is the conviction of things not seen. We cannot see the Lord, angels or evil forces but we are convinced that they are there.

Finally, faith is trusting God in His Word. Here we find that the object of our faith is not our faith, but God. If God has made a promise, then to trust in that promise is to trust in the One who made the promise. It is said that, "Faith is a response to the revealed will of God." **The key word is "revealed." If God has not said anything, then what is there to believe? Faith, then, is taking God at His Word.**

Let's say you are praying for someone to be supernaturally healed. Perhaps this person is close and dear to you and you would give your life to see healing come to them. You try to believe; you work on and muster all the faith you can, you greatly desire to see it. Desire, however, is not the same as faith. My question to you is this: "Has God promised you that your loved one will be healed?" There are several instances in the Bible about healing. Jesus and the disciples healed many. There are also miracles of this type in the Old Testament. But these are "descriptive" passages. They describe something that happened, but is not necessarily going to happen every time. In Acts 3, Peter and John saw a lame man and said to him, *"Silver and gold have I none; but such as I have give I thee: In the name of Jesus Christ of Nazareth rise up and walk." (KJV)* That happened, but it does not mean that every time you quote that verse someone will be healed. Later I'll address the "prescriptive" verses about healing found in James 5:13-16.

God has made promises, but the question is, "Has He written a promise on your heart?" If God has not placed a promise on your heart consistent with God's Word, then what is there to believe? Guilt on your part for lack of faith is totally inappropriate. Holding God accountable or becoming angry with His lack of action is unfair and detrimental to your Christian walk.

"Faith then means I have heard a promise from another and I trust in their character and capability to fulfill that promise." So, where do we get this faith? All faith in God comes from God.

One of many passages that indicate this is Romans 1:18, 19 which tells us, *"For the wrath of God is revealed from heaven against all ungodliness and unrighteousness of men who suppress the truth in unrighteousness, because that which is known about God is evident within them; for God made it evident to them."* Even those who have never heard, receive a measure of belief. God has placed it in their hearts. James 1:17 says, *"Every good thing given and every perfect gift is from above, coming down from the Father of lights, with whom there is no variation or shifting shadow."* Faith is definitely one of those good things.

This faith is not forced upon us. We have the choice to receive or reject faith as God offers it to us. In the parable of the sower Jesus says,

> "Listen to this! Behold, the sower went out to sow; as he was sowing, some seed fell beside the road, and the birds came and ate it up. Other seed fell on the rocky ground where it did not have much soil; and immediately it sprang up because it had no depth of soil. And after the sun had risen, it was scorched; and because it had no root, it withered away. Other seed fell among the thorns, and the thorns came up and choked it, and it yielded no crop. Other seeds fell into the good soil, and as they grew up and increased, they yielded a crop and produced thirty, sixty, and à hundredfold." And He was saying, "He who has ears to hear, let him hear." (Mark 4:3-9)

Jesus says in Mark 4:13, *"Do you not understand this parable? How will you understand all the parables?"* He is saying that the key to understanding the parables is to understand this particular parable. Jesus then interprets it for us:

"The sower sows the Word. These are the ones who are beside the road where the Word is sown; and when they hear, immediately Satan comes and takes away the Word which has been sown in them. In a similar way these are the ones on whom seed was sown on the rocky places, who, when they hear the Word, immediately receive it with joy; and they have no firm root in themselves, but are only temporary; then, when affliction or persecution arises because of the Word, immediately they fall away. And others are the ones on whom seed was sown among the thorns; these are the ones who have heard the Word, but the worries of the world, and the deceitfulness of riches, and the desires for other things enter in and choke the Word, and it becomes unfruitful. And those are the ones on whom seed was sown on the good soil; and they hear the Word and accept it and bear fruit, thirty, sixty, and a hundredfold." (Mark 4:14-20)

The sower is the one who proclaims and teaches God's Word. The seed is the Word of God. The different kinds of soils represent the hearts of people in relationship to what they do with the sower's offer of the seed or Word. Three reject God's Word—only the last type of soil receives the Word. (Some may argue that the third type of soil also receives, but greenery is not the sign for spiritual life in the Scripture; fruit is.)

The parable of the sower teaches that God wants us to have His Word, but it is our choice to receive faith through His Word. Romans 10:17 says, *"So faith comes from hearing, and hearing by the word of Christ."* The way we acquire faith is through His Word. Therefore, we have the choice to receive or reject the faith He offers to us. But who or what is our faith in?

THE DIRECTION OF BELIEVING PRAYER

All of us possess faith. We climb into our car each morning trusting it will start. We take medication our doctor has prescribed without thought. The difference in faith is often simply the object of that faith.

In Psalm 20:7, the Psalmist declares: "*Some boast in chariots and some in horses, but we will boast in the name of the LORD, our God.*" Chariots represent manpower—the things man has made. Horses represent wealth that we have accumulated. The Psalmist declares that he will not trust in the things of man, but in God.

Often in the Old Testament we find prayers beginning with praise and adoration to God. I think we start our prayers in the same fashion thinking we are flattering or "buttering up" God or bracing Him for the "killer prayer request." The saints of the Old Testament began in praise to remind themselves just how great God is and this increased their faith.

So, who is this God we worship? The Bible speaks of the attributes of God or the characteristics attributed to Him. Among them are:

1. God is omniscient or all-knowing (Psalm 139:1-6)

2. God is omnipresent or everywhere at once (Psalm 139:7-12)

3. God is Holy (Revelation 4:8)

4. God is just (Isaiah 30:18)

5. God is gracious (James 4:6)

6. God is sovereign—He is the ruler of the universe (I Chronicles 29:11, 12)

7. God is faithful (Lamentations 3:22, 23)

Perhaps the two attributes most crucial to our faith are that God is all loving (John 3:16) and that He is omnipotent (all powerful). **In other words, when we pray we want to know two things: Does God love me enough to answer my prayer and is God powerful enough to deliver?**

As we analyze our feelings about unanswered prayers, I think we will discover that we either feel that God does not care enough to answer or He is not capable of answering. To illustrate this point, I recall preaching at a revival in a South Georgia church when I was young. My pastor friend and I frequented the local diner that week to eat and invite people to the revival meetings. The owner of the diner shared with me about her teenage grandson dying. Her loss was recent and she was searching for answers. Rather than believe that God didn't love her, she chose to believe He was not able to help her.

God does love us. Yes, He loves us more than we could ever love ourselves. In Romans 8:31-32, the apostle Paul declares, *"What then shall we say to these things? If God is for us, who is against us? He who did not spare His own Son, but delivered Him over for us all, how will He not also with Him freely give us all things?"* God gave us His own Son on the cross, proving His love for us. *"But God demonstrates His own love toward us, in that while we were yet sinners, Christ died for us."* (Romans 5:8)

God is also all-powerful. There is nothing He cannot do within His perfections. Every now and then, I have an opportunity to share my faith with an atheist. Most try to win an argument by asking such questions as, "Can God make a rock so big He cannot pick it up?" When anyone asks a question like that, I know they are beginning with the wrong definition of all-powerfulness. God cannot sin; God cannot make a round square—these are not within his perfections. God can do anything within His perfections.[2]

God does have a plan and a will for each one of us. In the next chapter I will talk about this. Suffice to say for now, that we trust a God who is worthy of trust. The late African American preacher, S.M. Lockridge elaborated on God's trustworthiness in his message, "You Can Trust Him."[3]

> He's the one who made you, it is He who made us and not we ourselves. The heavens declare the glory of God and the firmament shows His handiwork. No means or measure can define His limitless love and no farseeing telescope can bring into visibility the coastline of His shoreless supply. *I'M TELLING YOU TODAY YOU CAN TRUST HIM.* (AMEN)
>
> No barrier can hinder Him from pouring out His blessing. He's enduringly strong and He's entirely sincere. He's eternally steadfast and He's immortally graceful. He's imperially powerful and He's impartially merciful. He's the greatest phenomenon that has ever crossed the horizon of this world. He's God's Son, He's the sinner's Savior, He's the centerpiece of civilization. *I'M TRYING TO TELL YOU CHURCH, YOU CAN TRUST HIM!* (AMEN)
>
> He does not have to call for help and you can't confuse Him. He doesn't need you and He doesn't need me. He stands alone in the solitude of Himself. He's awesome and He's unique. He's unparalleled, He's unprecedented, He's supreme, He's preeminent, He's the loftiest idea in literature, He's the highest personality in philosophy, He's the supreme problem of higher criticism, He's the fundamental doctrine of true theology, He's the cardinal necessity of spiritual religion, He's the miracle

of the age, He's the superlative of everything good you can call Him. *I'M TRYING TO TELL YOU CHURCH, YOU CAN TRUST HIM!* (AMEN)

He can satisfy all your needs, and He can do it simultaneously. He supplies strength for the weak and He's available for the tempted and the tried. He sympathizes and He sees. He guards and He guides, He heals the sick, He cleansed the Leper, He forgives sinners, He discharges debtors, He delivers the captives, He defends the feeble, He blesses the young, He regards the aged, He rewards the diligent, He beautifies the meek, *I'M TRYING TO TELL YOU CHURCH, YOU CAN TRUST HIM!* (AMEN)

He's the key to knowledge, He's the well spring of wisdom, He's the doorway of deliverance, He's the pathway of peace, He's the roadway of righteousness, He's the highway of holiness, He's the gateway to glory, *YOU CAN TRUST IN HIM!*

He's the master of the mighty, He's the captain of the conquers, He's the head of heroes, He's the leader of legislators, He's the overseer of the overcomers, He's the governor of the governors, He's the Prince of princes, He's the King of kings, He's the Lord of lords, *YOU... CAN... TRUST... HIM!!!*

His office is manifold, His promise is sure, His life is matchless, His goodness is limitless, His mercy is everlasting, His love never changes, His Word is enough, His grace is sufficient, His reign is righteous, His yoke is easy, His burden is light, I wish I could describe Him to you, He's indescribable because He's incomprehensible, He's irresistible because He's invincible. You can't get Him off your hands, you can't get Him off your mind, you can't outlive Him and you can't live without Him. Pilate couldn't stand it when he found he couldn't stop Him, and Pilate couldn't find any fault in Him. And the witnesses couldn't get their testimonies to agree and Herod couldn't kill Him, and death couldn't handle Him and thank God the grave couldn't hold Him. (AMEN)

There was nobody before Him and there will be nobody after Him. He has no predecessor, He'll have no successor, you can't impeach Him and He's not going to resign. *YOU CAN TRUST HIM!!!*

God does love you enough to help you. God is powerful enough to deliver on His promises. **You can trust Him!**

THE DYNAMICS OF BELIEVING PRAYER

How then can your faith grow? If the single greatest ingredient in getting God to say *yes* is your faith, then that should be a priority in your life. Let me suggest four things. First, you must stay in God's Word. *"So faith comes from hearing, and hearing by the word of Christ." (Romans 10:17)* The more you read the Bible, the more you will know about God. The more you know about God, the more you can trust Him. This principle is true in other relationships as well. When my wife, Pam, and I were first married, I trusted her and she trusted me. After all, we vowed to trust one another and abandon all others. However, I trust her much more today as I grow to know her better and see her trustworthiness. As we read the Bible we begin to better understand the heart and ways of God. As we grow deeper in our relationship we will not only trust Him more in the adventures of life, but also in our prayers.

The Bible gives us daily strength and nourishment. The key to growing in Christ is presented in Colossians 2:6, *"Therefore as you have received Christ Jesus the Lord, so walk in Him."* When I received Jesus, I met Him. The way to walk with Jesus is to meet Him every day. This is commonly referred to as a devotional or quiet time. Relying on a Sunday message from your pastor to completely nourish you is like relying on one meal a week to keep you strong. I recall in my first pastorate, I would eat a big meal every Sunday after church. If I was not invited to dine elsewhere, I would go to Mrs. Wilbanks' home for lunch. Mrs. Wilbanks and family would put on a great meal which any unmarried pastor would appreciate. As good as those meals were, I would be hungry again the next day. I did not need a huge meal every day, but I did need to eat. Your pastor may lay out a spiritual feast every Sunday, but you need to be in God's Word for nourishment and strength every day.

Second, in order to grow in our faith, we need some success in our prayer life. In order to do this, we need to know God's will. The only way you can exercise faith is to believe in the revealed will of God. God must first reveal something to you. (I will address this further in the next chapter.)

Third, you must rest in the ways of God. The Bible says,

> "For My thoughts are not your thoughts, nor are your ways My ways," declares the LORD. For as the heavens are higher than the earth, so are My ways higher than your ways and My thoughts than your thoughts."
> (Isaiah 55:8, 9)

We must trust God before the answer to prayer comes—regardless of the answer. I discovered that one of the primary reasons people refuse to come to Christ is that they are bitter against God.

Their bitterness often stems from unanswered prayers. Television mogul, Ted Turner, once expressed that he considered going into the ministry as a young man. Then his sister got cancer and in spite of his prayers, God never healed her. He said he refused to serve a God who didn't care enough to answer the most important request of his life.[4] Many struggle in the same way.

Know that God loves you and wants to bless your life. However, sometimes you do not get a *yes* answer. What happens then? Are you going to become angry with God? If your unanswered prayer hurts your relationship with Him, then your request was more important to you than your relationship with God. You must be willing to honor God and accept His will and His ways before your faith can grow to maturity.

Lastly, we must ask. James 4:2 says, *"...You do not have because you do not ask."* Asking is an act of faith. It is saying, "In spite of my doubts, I humbly come to you and ask for your help." God is honored when we ask because He is honored by faith. Sometimes we don't ask because we feel it is futile. We pray for years and our prayer is not answered, but remember, sometimes God says to *wait*.

I grew up near Athens, Georgia in a little town called Bogart. I attended Sunday School at Bogart First Baptist Church and for the first ten years I was not a believer. Year after year I witnessed my classmates and friends make decisions for Christ. As a 16 year old, I was still not a believer; neither was my 13 year old brother, nor my dad who was 42. One winter night as I lay in bed, I wrestled with God calling me to salvation. I had waited so long I felt God might run out of patience with me so that night I gave my heart to Christ. A few weeks later my brother and I professed Christ openly at church and before the invitation was finished, my dad also came forward to receive Christ.

I share this story because of what took place in that little church after my profession. It is customary in Baptist churches for those who make a decision to be greeted by the church members after the service has ended. What took place stunned me. Since I had attended the church for many years, I felt people would be surprised that I was not already a Christian and I wondered if anyone really cared that much. Yet, one by one, the people came by to shake my hand and hug me as they rejoiced in my decision. Many could not hold back their tears. My second grade teacher, Mrs. McLeroy, hugged me and said, "You don't know how long I have been praying for you."

As I looked back, my life suddenly started making sense. For years I had refused to receive Christ because I wanted to run my own life. By most standards I was not a bad kid, but I guess it was the hope of doing something bad in the future that kept me from God. But when freedom came, something would not allow me to do the things I thought I wanted to do. In fact, I had a strong awareness of God in spite of my lost condition. One might say I always felt God's hand on my life. At the age of 16, I could not take my double-mindedness any longer. That night in my room I felt I had to decide for Christ or I might forever lose my opportunity. Weeks later as I stood in front of the altar after my profession of faith, I finally understood. It was the prayers of my family, my friends and my church that had paved my path. Mrs. McLeroy's faithful prayers were finally answered. I am thankful she and others like her never gave up on me. **God does not give up on His people or on their prayers.** *"And without faith it is impossible to please Him, for he who comes to God must believe that He is and that He is a rewarder of those who seek Him." (Hebrews 11:6)*
But how do I know God's will?

DIRECTION: COMMITTED TO GOD'S WILL

CHAPTER 3

DIRECTION: COMMITTED TO GOD'S WILL

Knowing the will of God is often difficult. Rick Pughe came on staff at First Baptist Oviedo in the summer of 1996. He and his wife, Gina, had three children. The oldest was an eight year old boy named Chad. Chad was a great kid with a tender heart. He had been through a great deal of adversity having been previously diagnosed and treated for leukemia. At the time Rick came on staff as our College Pastor, Chad's disease was in remission. A few years later the disease came back with a vengeance.

Rick and Gina did everything they could for their son, including a bone marrow transplant. I remember soon after the procedure, visiting them at Shands Hospital in Gainesville, Florida. My heart was broken for Chad. The transplant had caused him great discomfort and pain and he was just trying to hang on. As the nurses attended to Chad, Rick and I, along with two other men from our church went down to the cafeteria.

It seems like yesterday (it's been over ten years now) that Rick looked across the table at me and confessed that it seemed God was preparing him. He felt God was speaking to his heart and God would soon take Chad home. One of the other men quickly jumped in and said that Rick needed to stay positive and believe God. I then looked at Rick and asked, "Tell me what God has been saying to you." God was speaking to my friend's heart and preparing him for something he did not want. It wasn't the *yes* answer he had been seeking, but it was nevertheless God speaking.

Within a few weeks Chad was with the Lord. It was one of the most difficult and saddest experiences of my ministry. Even as I write about it, my heart relives the emotion I felt during that time. We don't know all the answers to why and never will on this side of heaven. However, God did speak. Sometimes He speaks to our hearts and gives us an answer we do not want to hear. We shun the answer as though "it's of the devil" or our negative emotion—but sometimes it's God. John Maxwell has said, "*Sometimes we know the will of God we just don't have the courage to do it.*" [1] Sometimes we also hear from God and know His will but do not have the courage to listen.

There are times we want God to do something simple. Other times we want to see the miraculous and sensational. But the question is always the same, "What did God say?" What did He actually promise?

Another friend of mine (name withheld) once shared a story of what he thought was a step of faith. While he was in college, the president of his school passed away. The president was a fine Christian gentleman and one who consistently walked with the Lord. My friend was a spiritual leader on campus and felt God laid it on his heart to pray that the president would rise from the dead before his burial. He believed that this bodily resurrection would be a great testimony and cause revival to break out on campus.

He and his friends recruited prayer warriors all around campus to pray as he and others confidently proclaimed to the student body that this miracle would take place.

Even at the gravesite he did not give up hope. However, no amount of praying or mustering up of faith could change the fact that the president was dead and was not coming back from heaven. My friend later admitted his great embarrassment to me—he was crushed. How do you ever really recover from a disappointment like that?

Two friends—two stories: one who knew the will of God, but found it difficult to hear it; the other convinced he knew it, but did not. You see from these stories that the will of God has a prominent place in our prayer lives. But you may ask, "How do I really know the will of God? Isn't His will restrictive? Isn't *if it be Thy will* tacked onto prayer just to cover our lack of faith?"

I John 5:14, 15 gives us great insight.

> "This is the confidence which we have before Him, that, if we ask anything according to His will, He hears us. And if we know that He hears us in whatever we ask, we know that we have the requests which we have asked from Him."

As the apostle John neared the end of his life, he looked back. In his wisdom and under the Spirit's inspiration, he looked at some of the assurances we have in life. In verse 13 he explained that we have assurance of salvation: *"These things I have written to you who believe in the name of the Son of God, so that you may know that you have eternal life."* Then in verses 14 and 15 he wrote to us about assurance in prayer. The word *know* is used 26 times in this little book. He wants us to *know* that God is there for us at every turn of life—including in our prayers.

Before we look at how to discern God's will, we must first observe our attitude and perspective toward His will. **Rather than seeing the will of God as being restrictive, why can't we see it as liberating?**

THE POTENTIAL WITHIN THE WILL OF GOD

In I John 5:14 we read the word confidence which comes from a Greek word meaning *freedom of speech* and there it implies verbal confidence to come before God and speak. It also suggests the idea of bold access.

Because of what Jesus did on the cross, we now have total access to God. Matthew 27:51 tells us that as Jesus died on the cross, God ripped the veil of the temple in half signifying the believers' access to the throne of God. Hebrews 10:19 says, *"Since therefore, brethren, we have confidence to enter the holy place by the blood of Jesus..."* We now can enter and have an audience with God with full confidence—freedom of prayer or speech. I John 5:14 goes on to tell us that *"We know that if we ask anything according to His will, He hears us, and if we know that He hears us in whatever we ask, we know that we have the requests which we have asked from Him."*

The word, know is the Greek word *oida* meaning to know factually. The absolute truth is that we know if we pray according to His will, He will hear us and if He hears us, He will say *yes* to our prayers. A similar thought is expressed by Jesus in the gospel of John.

> "Whatever you ask in My name, that will I do, so that the Father may be glorified in the Son. If you ask Me anything in My name, I will do it." (John 14:13, 14)

Many of us end our prayers with "in Jesus' name." However, there is not one prayer in the Bible that ends this way. So, what does this verse mean?

Let me illustrate it this way: The signature or name on something is significant. When the authors of the Declaration of Independence signed their names to that historic document they not only ratified it, they placed their name behind it. When we pray in Jesus' name, we are placing His signature on the prayer. Praying in Jesus' name then means that we are praying for that which He is behind or is in His will. Therefore, "...*whatever you ask in My name, that will I do, that the Father may be glorified in the Son.*" When we pray in the will of God—things that He can place His signature on—He answers with *yes* and it brings glory to Him. **The will of God is not a limitation but an opportunity for God to bring Himself glory and for us to be blessed.** If we say that the will of God is restrictive it's like saying that the Atlantic Ocean is restrictive to a minnow.

Just because God will close the door on things that are not the best for us or would not bring glory to Him does not mean it's bad news. When I was growing up, we often looked through the Sears catalog to make our wish list for Christmas. We had to find what we wanted in the catalog and then order it through the mail. Of course, Sears did not sell everything. For example, if we wanted to buy a new car we wouldn't find one in the catalog to order. Was that a reason to be upset with Sears? No, because there were many other things we could choose from. There were thousands of items available through the catalog. Sears sold more things than we could ever buy. Likewise, God offers more blessings than we can ever handle. In fact, **God wants to give us what we would want if we were wise**

enough to want it. We merely need to walk with God, know His will, and then ask. Yet the will of God seems to be a mystery to the human mind. It's like a puzzle that few can understand.

THE PUZZLE OF THE WILL OF GOD

The promise in I John 5:14, 15 is great and irrevocable but there is one word that gives us all problems—*if.* *"If we ask anything according to His will..."* Why would your request not be in the will of God if you want it or feel like you need it? Maybe God has a *better* plan. God, in His foreknowledge and wisdom, can see the big picture and we cannot.

In the film "Bruce Almighty," the main character was critical of God so He allowed Bruce to be God for a few weeks. Bruce became so overwhelmed by the prayers of people ringing in his head that he finally said yes to all of them. Of course, the results were chaotic.

Garth Brooks wrote a song entitled "Thank God for Unanswered Prayers." The song is about how a young man had prayed to marry a certain girl. When he met up with her again years later and compared her to the wonderful woman he did marry, he was grateful that God had not answered that prayer. Can God answer every prayer with a *yes* answer? How can one man pray for dry weather for his golf game, and another in the same town pray for rain for his crops and both have their prayer answered?

You have heard the phrase "Be careful what you pray for." Well, there's a story of a young man who went big game hunting. As he was walking through the jungle, he tripped and fell down a short hill. As he looked up he saw a lion in the distance coming straight at him. Unable to reach his rifle, he cried out to God, "Lord, please let this lion be a Christian lion." Just then the lion stopped in his tracks a few feet from the man. The lion got on his knees and prayed, "Lord, thank you for this food I am about to receive."

God sometimes says *no* because in His wisdom there is something *bigger* in His overall plan. As I was graduating from seminary, my wife and I were praying about where God would want us in ministry. A church in my hometown needed a pastor so we prayed asking God to open that door. Although I had been recommended there, the search committee was so diligent in their preparation that by the time they contacted us with an offer we had already received a call to plant a church near Atlanta, Georgia. Had I gone to that hometown church, I know my life would have taken a different turn but I believe God led me down a better path.

Then too, God may say *no* because there is something *binding* His overall plan. The Bible teaches, *"...and whatever we ask we receive from Him, because we keep His commandments and do the things that are pleasing in His sight." (I John 3:22)* There may be many prayers God wants to answer in your life, but sin is binding these answers. In the following chapter, I will address the necessity of being clean before God.

I said that the will of God is liberating, not restrictive, and I have addressed the mystery of His will. But how can you discover God's will as you pray?

THE PRESCRIPTION FOR FINDING THE WILL OF GOD

Matthew 7:7, 8 reads, *"Ask, and it will be given to you; seek, and you will find; knock, and it will be opened to you. For everyone who asks receives and he who seeks finds, and to him who knocks it will be opened."*

These verses teach us that when we know God's will, we simply need to ask. When we do not know God's will we ask our desires, but we also seek to know God's will in the matter. Then we keep on knocking until the door is opened; that is, we have a peace in our heart that we know His will and our prayer is as good as answered.

Dr. Henry Blackaby, author of "Experiencing God," wrote, *"If the Christian does not know when God is speaking, he is in trouble at the heart of his Christian life."* While that is true, I must admit that hearing from God has not always been easy for me. In fact, the number one question asked of me in my years of ministry is "How can I know God's will for my life?" So, where do we begin?

1. You must **desire** the will of God. Are you walking in His will now? Do you want His will more than your *yes* answer to prayer? Often we rationalize situations and talk ourselves into believing something is God's will when it is not. Author and conference speaker, Dr. Ray Stedman tells the story of a young lady's outlook on her upcoming marriage:

> "Dear God. I can hardly believe that this is my wedding day. I know I haven't been able to spend much time with You lately, with all the rush of getting ready for today, and I'm sorry. I guess, too, that I feel a little guilty when I try to pray about all this, since Larry still isn't a Christian. But oh, Father, I love him so much, what else can I do? I just couldn't give him up. Oh, You must save him, some way, somehow. You know how much I've prayed for him, and the way we've discussed the gospel together. I've tried not to appear too religious, I know, but that's because I didn't want to scare him off. Yet he isn't antagonistic and I can't

understand why he hasn't responded. Oh, if he only were a Christian.

Dear Father, please bless our marriage. I don't want to disobey You, but I do love him and I want to be his wife, so please be with us and please don't spoil my wedding day."[3]

That sounds like a sincere, earnest prayer, doesn't it? But if it is stripped of its fine, pious language, what is it really saying? Stedman interprets:

"Dear Father, I don't want to disobey You, but I must have my own way at all costs. For I love what You do not love, and I want what You do not want. So please be a good God and deny Yourself, and move off Your throne, and let me take over. If You don't like this, then all I ask is that You bite Your lip and say or do nothing that will spoil my plans, and let me enjoy myself."[4]

Many can identify with this young lady who wanted her way in spite of God's plan for her life.

Several years after I began pastoring a church in the Atlanta area, I was fortunate enough to have a very sharp young man become my pastoral intern. We met each week for a mentoring time and he helped minister in the church. Eventually he joined our staff as youth pastor. Several months into this assignment he was offered and accepted another job at a larger church. I know he thought I would rejoice with him for this opportunity, but I was not in a rejoicing mood. For a period of time our church had been steadily growing, but then the community began to change and it seemed I was saying goodbye to a key family every month. I found myself upset with God. I felt I was working hard and seeing little fruit. Now God was taking away the man I had trained for ministry and I was going to be in this by myself.

As I prayed about it, the Lord revealed to me that I was in disagreement with His will for my life. I was in conflict with Him. If we are honest with ourselves, every time we get upset with God, we are in disagreement with His will. Until we get our wills in harmony with His, it's going to be difficult to hear from Him. Desiring God's will in prayer falls under the same principle. Do we want God's will more than a healing, more than a financial need met, more than success?

2. We must **hear** from God. As I said before, there are two basic ways that we hear from God: the first is through the Bible and the second is through prayer. Both are prompted by the indwelling of the Spirit of God. Paul prayed this for the church at Colossae, *"For this reason also, since the day we heard of it, we have not ceased to pray for you and to ask that you may be filled with the knowledge of His will in all spiritual wisdom and understanding," (Colossians 1:9)*

As we search the Scripture for God's will, we must realize that there are thousands of promises in the Bible. The Spirit of God speaks to our heart as we read the Scripture. Let me emphasize that His promptings will not be out of context nor contradict the Bible, in part or as a whole, because the Holy Spirit inspired the Scripture. II Timothy 3:16 says, *"All Scripture is inspired by God and profitable for teaching, for reproof, for correction, for training in righteousnes..."* The Greek word is *theopneutos* means God inspired or **God breathed**. It is the Scriptures themselves that are inspired by God and therefore perfect and authoritative to our lives.

Scripture teaches that all of God's promises are *yes* to us. Have you claimed a promise lately? Years ago as I was pastoring my first church, I was struggling in my heart on whether to stay at the church I loved or move to Ft. Worth to attend seminary. Proverbs 21:31 kept coming back to me. *"The horse is prepared for the day of battle..."* Well, I knew I wasn't a horse, so how could that apply to me? Yet, God used this Scripture to speak to me. Like the horse, I was going to be facing my battles in the ministry. I needed all the preparation and knowledge available to me. A few months later Pam and I were on the road to seminary. It would prove to be one of the toughest but best decisions we ever made.

God not only speaks through Scripture—He also speaks through prayer. We often see prayer as a monologue rather than a dialogue. Have you ever carried on a one-way conversation on the phone and had to ask your party, "Are you still there?" Sometimes our prayers are like that. We do all the talking and never give God a chance to speak. Prayer is not only talking to God, but also listening to Him.

In a sense there is a cycle of prayer. The cycle begins in heaven with a desire in God's heart. Then the Father communicates His desire through His Spirit to our hearts. Third, we pray according to the Spirit's guidance. *"But you, beloved, building yourselves up on your most holy faith, praying in the Holy Spirit," (Jude 20).* Lastly, the Father hears and answers our prayers.

When my children were young I wanted them to have a puppy. When I was growing up I had a dog and felt that my kids should have the same opportunity. My wife was not as excited about the idea, knowing she would end up being the caretaker. However, I knew she would go along with the idea if the kids wanted it badly enough. The trouble was they never mentioned wanting a puppy.

There was a puppy store in the mall we frequented so I made it a habit every few weeks to take them in that store. Occasionally, I would ask the clerk to take a puppy out of the crate and let our kids play with it. After several weeks of this, they wanted a puppy so badly that we as parents could not say no.

This is how God often works in our lives. As we commit and listen to Him, He changes our desires to coincide with His by slowly revealing to us the things He wants for our lives. Sometimes this comes in the form of a prayer burden. The cycle of prayer begins as He lays His will on our hearts.

Earlier I shared with you the story of my healing from diabetes. The prayer began in heaven and God laid it on my heart as He revealed His will to me. God can and will speak to your heart too—through His Word and in prayer.

Why would Henry Blackaby say that not hearing from God is a reflection on our relationship with Him? I believe when our relationship with God is not close, we do not recognize His voice when He is speaking. When a loved one calls you on the phone, you immediately recognize their voice. My kids give me a hard time when I call them and say, "This is dad," because they know who it is. On the other hand, I hate it when someone I barely know calls and says, "This is Jim." As a Pastor I may know 50 Jims so I spend the rest of the conversation trying to figure out who this Jim is. The reason is that I have not spent enough time talking to Jim to recognize his voice. Most Christians are like this with God. **We do not listen everyday to get direction on less important matters in our lives, so when the big issues arrive, we can't discern God's voice over our own or the devil's.**

The key to praying God's will is a consistent walk with God.

I challenge you to have a devotional time with God everyday to shape your life and sharpen His voice in your heart. It will lead to a multitude of answered prayers.

A WORD OF ENCOURAGEMENT

There are times in my life when I pray without knowing God's will. What then? First, the Bible teaches to keep on praying or "knocking." The worst that can happen is He will say *no*. However, the Bible also teaches that, *"If we delight ourselves in the Lord, He will give us the desires of our heart."* My challenge to you is to keep on delighting in the Lord. Make Him the delight of your life—make His will the delight of your heart. Pray as Jesus prayed in the garden *"...yet not as I will, but as You will."* *(Matthew 26:39)*

In another encouraging word, Scripture says:

> "In the same way the Spirit also helps our weakness; for we do not know how to pray as we should, but the Spirit Himself intercedes for us with groanings too deep for words; and He who searches the hearts knows what the mind of the Spirit is, because He intercedes for the saints according to the will of God". (Romans 8:26, 27)

Some take this text as proof of "a prayer language" or "speaking in tongues." These are *groanings* that no one can understand and they are prayers for every Christian, not just those who possess a certain gift. These verses teach that there are times when we do not know God's will and that even when our spirit is not in tune with the Holy Spirit, the Holy Spirit prays for us *"according to the will of God."*

If we know God's will and our prayer begins in heaven, how could God not say *yes*? But there is a third key to getting God to say *yes*. It has to do with our inner life.

Devotion: Forgiven through God's Grace

CHAPTER 4

DEVOTION: FORGIVEN THROUGH GOD'S GRACE

The normal Christian life should be one with consistent *yes* answers to prayer. I have talked about three possible answers to prayer: *yes, no,* and *wait.* But there is a fourth possibility—God will not answer at all. Scripture teaches,

> "Behold, the LORD'S hand is not so short that it cannot save; nor is His ear so dull that it cannot hear. But your iniquities have made a separation between you and your God, and your sins have hidden His face from you so that He does not hear." (Isaiah 59:1, 2)

I was sharing Christ with a lady several years ago. After listening for only a few minutes, she snapped back at me that she had prayed for God to save her marriage but He didn't. She was not going to follow a God who ignored the most important prayer of her life.

Certainly we can understand and identify with this lady's heartbreak. I wanted to ask, "Were you in the will of God when you prayed those prayers? Were you following Christ? Was He Lord of your life?" I knew her situation and I knew her answers would be no to these questions. How do we expect God to answer our prayer if we are not walking with Him? What role does sin and rebellion play in our prayer lives? Is there a time when God does not hear our prayers?

The apostle John writes to the church about assurances. He teaches us about love in action and then applies this to our prayer life.

> "But whoever has the world's goods, and sees his brother in need and closes his heart against him, how does the love of God abide in him? Little children, let us not love with word or with tongue, but in deed and truth. We will know by this that we are of the truth, and will assure our heart before Him in whatever our heart condemns us; for God is greater than our heart and knows all things. Beloved, if our heart does not condemn us, we have confidence before God; and whatever we ask we receive from Him, because we keep His commandments and do the things that are pleasing in His sight." (I John 3:17-22)

In Chapter 3 we discovered that if we pray in the will of God, we are ready for a *yes* answer. Yet, why is God sometimes still silent? Very simply, something is wrong in the life of the person who is praying.

THE BINDING OF OUR PRAYERS

If we are not right with God, He will not hear our prayers with the intention of answering them. Psalm 66:18 says, *"If I regard wickedness in my heart, The Lord will not hear..."* The word regard comes from a Hebrew word that means to *cherish* something. The idea is that we hold on tightly, playing our sin over and over in our minds like a video. When we will not let go of sin, we are regarding it in our hearts and God will not hear our prayer.

Since God is omniscient (knows everything) and is omnipresent (everywhere at once), He hears everything. This verse means that God will not give our prayer a hearing. He will not hear in the sense that He will answer. Isaiah says that our sins cause us to be separated from God.

To better understand this principle let's remember the story of Adam and Eve. After creation they were in close fellowship with God. Genesis 3:8 says, *"They (Adam and Eve) heard the sound of the Lord walking in the garden..."* Since there does not seem to be a surprise element, we can only assume that God and Adam talked together frequently. After Adam sinned, an immediate separation took place and a curse fell on all mankind. God killed animals and used the skins to cover Adam and Eve with clothing to remind them of their shame and separation from Him. The death of the animals would forever remind them that death would be the result of their sin.

The Bible teaches that God does not take sin lightly. Romans 6:23 says, *"the wages of sin is death."* The wage or payment for sin is death. Death is not annihilation (we will all live forever somewhere); death is separation. When we die, our soul and spirit are separated from our body and if we die without our sins being forgiven we will spend eternity separated from God.

God takes sin so seriously that He sent His Son, Jesus Christ, to die on the cross for our sin. *"For God so loved the world, that He gave His only begotten Son, that whoever believes in Him shall not perish, but have eternal life." (John 3:16)* In Revelation 21:1 the Bible teaches that no sin will enter into heaven.

Once we receive Christ into our heart as Savior and Lord (Romans 10:9, 10), we begin a new relationship with God. At that moment we also have fellowship with Him. Sometimes we do not walk with Christ as we should. I John 1:8 says, *"If we say that we have no sin, we are deceiving ourselves and the truth is not in us."* Therefore, we must confess those sins to God. *"If we confess our sins, He is faithful and righteous to forgive us our sins and to cleanse us from all unrighteousness." (I John 1:9)*

When we regard unconfessed sin in our lives, our fellowship (not our relationship) with God is broken and at that moment we are no longer walking with God—we are in rebellion. **If God answered our prayers while we are in rebellion, it would only encourage us to rebel more.**

Parents can identify. At one time I was trying to help my son purchase a car. I found a car advertised in the newspaper that I thought would pique his interest. I called the seller and asked why he was selling the car. He replied "It's a car I bought for my daughter. Last week she came in at 4 o'clock in the morning. I am just not going to participate in that kind of lifestyle." What loving, concerned parent is going to condone behavior that will hurt their child? If God answers our prayers when we are in sin, He will be encouraging a life apart from an intimate walk with Him.

In his book, *"Why Prayers Are Unanswered,"* John Lavender retells the story of Norman Vincent Peale. When Peale was a little boy, he found a big black cigar; he slipped into an alley and lit it up. It did not taste good, but it made him feel really grown up. When he saw his father coming, he quickly put the cigar behind his back and tried to act casual. Desperate to divert his father's attention, Norman pointed to a billboard advertising a circus. "Can I go, Dad? Please let me go when the circus comes to town." His father's reply taught Norman a lesson he never forgot. He said quietly, but firmly, "Son, never make a petition, while at the same time trying to hide a smoldering disobedience."[1]

When we step out of God's will into disobedience, we step out of what I have referred to as God's path of blessing. This is His place of blessing because it is walking in the path of God's will. Sin takes us away from God's will and therefore, the blessings and the answers to prayer that we desire.

The Bible says that in order to receive favor from God we must obey Him (I John 3:22). Sometimes we try to rationalize our disobedience. Life seems to be fine for a while, but God is patient and the payback for sin does not necessarily come everyday.

When I lived near Atlanta I had a beautiful weeping willow tree in my backyard. My dog would bite the tree and strip the bark off. One of my church members, who worked for a lawn service company, told me that unless something was done, the tree would die. He said that it might take a few years, but the insects would infest and eventually kill it. For two years the tree looked great; then by the third year it was completely dead. The damage had been done three years earlier but it took a while for death to show itself.

Sometimes we hide our disobedience by masking it and we think since it has no immediate consequences it must be fine with God. Then one day we realize our disobedience has destroyed our fellowship with God and our sin shuts His ears to our prayers. What are some of the things we need to watch for?

THE BARRIERS THAT WE FACE

Sometimes it helps to get specific. The Bible reveals several sins that cut our prayers off at the root.

1) Unbelief

> "But if any of you lacks wisdom, let him ask of God, who gives to all generously and without reproach, and it will be given to him. But he must ask in faith without any doubting, for the one who doubts is like the surf of the sea, driven and tossed by the wind. For that man ought not to expect that he will receive anything from the Lord..." (James 1:5-7)

When we think of unbelief we think of weakness rather than sin. However, when we do not believe God's promise, we are saying that God is lying to us. Faith and trust are foundational building blocks to our Christian life. Unbelief causes us to harden our heart against God. The Bible teaches,

> "Take care, brethren, that there not be in any one of you an evil, unbelieving heart that falls away from the living God. But encourage one another day after day, as long as it is still called "Today," so that none of you will be hardened by the deceitfulness of sin." (Hebrews 3:12, 13)

Then in the same chapter of Hebrews it says, "*So we see that they were not able to enter because of unbelief.*" *(Hebrews 3:19)* Their unbelief not only led to sin, it was sin.

All of us doubt God's promise at some point. Doubt, in a sense, is a part of faith. What is the difference between doubt and unbelief? Doubting faith says, "I'm not sure if this is going to work out, but I am going to obey God anyway." Unbelief says, "I don't know if this is going to work out so I will not do it; I will not obey God." The real difference is action. Doubting faith acts in spite of fear. Unbelief leads one to act in disobedience because the person believes they are better off trusting in their own judgment than following Christ.

If we are living outside of His will because of lack of trust, we will not believe God will answer our prayers. If our prayers require us to step out on faith and we refuse, our unbelief again will cause our prayers and those events connected to our prayers to be unfulfilled.

2) Wrong relationships with others is another reason our prayers go unanswered.

> "Therefore if you are presenting your offering at the altar, and there remember that your brother has something against you, leave your offering there before the altar and go; first be reconciled to your brother, and then come and present your offering." (Matthew 5:23, 24)

It is said, "You can't be right with God and be wrong with man." Romans 13:8 says, "*Owe nothing to anyone except to love one another; for he who loves his neighbor has fulfilled the law.*" When we sin against someone, we create a debt in their thinking toward us.[2] That is why people say things like, "I'm going to get even." Often when someone offends another, the offended one feels payment must be made. An apology is not enough; they want a "pound of flesh." The church is littered with bitter people who have never had their debts satisfied, who never get their "pound of flesh" and we wonder why God seems so far away.

Our Christian life is based on relationships. The Ten Commandments even point to this. The first four commandments concern our relationship with God and the final six, our relationships with people. If we have a problem with a brother we need to go to him, and him alone, and try to make it right. Matthew 18:15 says, *"If your brother sins, go and show him his fault in private; if he listens to you, you have won your brother."* This is not an option—it is a command.

3) A wrong relationship with our spouse

"You husbands in the same way, live with your wives in an understanding way, as with someone weaker, since she is a woman; and show her honor as a fellow heir of the grace of life, so that your prayers will not be hindered." (I Peter 3:7) The most precious relationship we have outside of Christ is the relationship with our spouse, since we are usually around them more than any other person. It is natural that Peter would single out the spousal relationship.

Although men are specifically mentioned, it's obvious this verse applies to both husband and wife. The first six verses of this chapter speak to wives about their relationship with their husbands. Verse seven brings in husbands and a summary statement of cause and effect, that is, if we are not right with our spouse our prayers will be hindered.

How many arguments have taken place? How many hurtful words have been said? How many hurts have been harbored in the heart?

Researcher George Barna's surveys indicate that there are as many divorces within the church as outside the church.[3] I have been pastoring for over 25 years and am amazed at the growing number of divorces within the church.

During the first six years of my ministry in a church outside Atlanta, we experienced no divorces. In the last three years of that ministry to a congregation of 325 people, we had two divorces and one of them came to us with previous marriage problems.

In the past 15 years, I have seen an ever-growing number of broken marriages within the church. Several years ago following a conversation with a man who had left his wife, I asked the Lord, "What is going on? What has changed in the past 15 to 20 years in the church?" As God was speaking to my heart, I realized that the secular worldview has crept in and now dominates the home life.

My personal library contains numerous books on the subject of the home. Older books address the roles of the husband and wife while the newer books don't. The new books have great insights and are worth reading, but virtually nothing is mentioned about spousal roles.

In I Peter 3, the chapter begins by teaching us that wives are to be submissive to their husbands.

> "In the same way, you wives, be submissive to your own husbands so that even if any of them are disobedient to the word, they may be won without a word by the behavior of their wives, as they observe your chaste and respectful behavior. Your adornment must not be merely external—braiding the hair, and wearing gold jewelry, or putting on dresses; but let it be the hidden person of the heart, with the imperishable quality of a gentle and quiet spirit, which is precious in the sight of God. For in this way in former times the holy women also, who hoped in God, used to adorn

themselves, being submissive to their own husbands; just as Sarah obeyed Abraham, calling him lord, and you have become her children if you do what is right without being frightened by any fear." (I Peter 3:1-6)

Many may be offended by these verses; however, as Bible-believing Christians, we know they are the Word of God. However, even if we say we believe them, some of us don't want a reminder.

The most popular passage about spousal roles is found in Ephesians 5.

"Wives, be subject to your own husbands, as to the Lord. For the husband is the head of the wife, as Christ also is the head of the church, He Himself being the Savior of the body. But as the church is subject to Christ, so also the wives ought to be to their husbands in everything. Husbands, love your wives, just as Christ also loved the church and gave Himself up for her, so that He might sanctify her, having cleansed her by the washing of water with the word, that He might present to Himself the church in all her glory, having no spot or wrinkle or any such thing; but that she would be holy and blameless. So husbands ought also to love their own wives as their own bodies. He who loves his own wife loves himself; for no one ever hated his own flesh, but nourishes and cherishes it, just as Christ also does the church, because we are members of His body. FOR THIS REASON A MAN SHALL LEAVE HIS FATHER AND MOTHER AND SHALL BE JOINED TO HIS WIFE, AND THE TWO SHALL BECOME ONE FLESH. This mystery is great; but I am speaking with reference to Christ and the church. Nevertheless, each individual among you also is to love his own wife even as himself, and the wife must see to it that she respects her husband." (Ephesians 5:22-33)

In this passage, we find that husbands are to be the leaders in everything. The husband is a symbol of Christ and the wife symbolizes the church. The Christian marriage is a beautiful picture of Christ's relationship to the church, but somehow we have lost this picture.

If I were to ask wives in our church if they are submissive, they would say yes and in most cases, their husbands would agree. If I asked the husbands if they are the leader in the home, most would also say yes. The problem is that we have lost the meaning of these roles in our culture.

Leader comes from the Greek word which means *to govern.* A leader by definition is a decision maker. In most homes today the decisions have largely been delegated to the wife and mother. After all, she is with the children more. Men get home from the pressure of work and are more than happy to delegate the everyday decisions to their wives. An interesting article in USA Today, "Women Rule the Roost, and that's OK with Men," reported some 1,260 couples were surveyed and in 43 percent of these couples the women made almost twice as many decisions as their husbands. Four major areas were included in the survey: planning weekends, household finances, major home purchases and TV viewing.[4]

Lead researcher Rick Morin said, *"I was surprised by the percentage of men who made none of those decisions in any of the areas. A significant percentage were just bystanders."* [5] Melinda Forthoter, Director of the Institute for Families in Society at the University of South Carolina, added that the men do not seem to mind. She says, *"...they're content to follow their partner's lead."* [6]

Few realize the consequences to this reversal of roles. Neither the wife nor the husband realizes that the manhood and respect are being torn out of the heart of the man. At best, his children begin to look at him as a separate entity in the family and at worst, an intruder. The less respect he gets from his wife and children the more apt he is to seek attention elsewhere. This often involves spending more time outside the home and sometimes establishing wrong relationships. The more time he spends away from home, the more distant his wife gets and the more independent she becomes. After all, according to the modern secular world view, this independence is a desirable objective. Consequently, the couple grows apart; their relationship and their prayers are hurt.

The heart of the problem is listening to the world—we allow television, movies, music and the media to form our views of life. In our world, leadership is exalted and being a helper is frowned upon as being inferior. Scripturally, however, the concept of the wife being the helper (Genesis 2) is the same as the Holy Spirit being our helper. The Holy Spirit is not inferior to the Son, nor the Son to the Spirit. They have different roles in the Godhead.

The wife is called alongside to help. This is the line of authority that God has set up in the home but it does not mean that the husband is more intelligent or that he is superior to the woman. Just as there is proper order and authority in the military, in the legal system and even in the corporate world, there is also proper authority in the home. When the husband is home, the wife should always refer even small decisions to him. The man should always put his family first in decision-making by gathering input from family members and then taking action. Men must assume this responsibility because decision making is a responsibility of leadership.

An additional word to husbands: Just as a wife should respect or admire her husband and look to him to lead, the husband must love his wife as Christ loves the church. Ephesians 5:29 says, *"...for no one ever hated his own flesh, but nourishes and cherishes it, just as Christ also does the church..."* The word cherish has to do with protecting, loving, making her feel that she is a precious and most important part of your life. Just as Christ cherishes us and puts us first, the husband is to put his wife before his own needs. In turn, this makes her admiration and submission to him easier.

I invite you to read and pray over I Peter 3:1-7 and Ephesians 5:22-33 and ask God to correct your heart and restore your relationship. **Put yourself in a position where your prayers will be answered and your life will be blessed.**

4) An unforgiving spirit

Perhaps the biggest reason our prayers go unanswered is because we harbor an unforgiving spirit. I touched on this earlier when I spoke about wrong relationships. However, this point is so significant it needs elaboration. In Matthew 6:14 and 15 Jesus said,

> "For if you forgive others for their transgressions, your heavenly Father will also forgive you. But if you do not forgive others, then your Father will not forgive your transgressions."

Forgiveness is referred to in Scripture on different levels. There is the forgiveness we receive at salvation and this forgiveness never ends. I am often asked, "What if a Christian commits a sin but dies before he has a chance to ask forgiveness. Is he still saved?" The answer is yes. When Jesus died, all our sins were in the future. If we had to be re-forgiven for salvation every time we sinned, Jesus would have to die over and over again (Hebrews 6). As believers, we need to ask forgiveness for our sins, not to be sure of our salvation, but to renew our fellowship with God.

The other level of forgiveness is forgiving others. If we harbor unforgiveness in our heart, our fellowship with God is broken and He will not answer our prayers. This side of forgiveness is tough, especially for those who have been wronged often and by many. However, when we refuse to forgive, a hardening process begins to take place in our hearts. It starts with a lack of forgiveness which turns to anger which then over time, turns to bitterness. Hebrews 12:15 says, *"See to it that no one comes short of the grace of God; that no root of bitterness springing up causes trouble, and by it many be defiled..."*

Few ever admit they are bitter. However, as I said, the church is littered with bitter people. I have counseled people over the years who were seething with anger. When I said, "You must deal with your bitterness," they replied defensively, "Oh, I'm not bitter!" Yet, anyone could see they were consumed with it.

Bitterness hurts the one who is bitter. Very often the one you are bitter against does not know it and really doesn't care. There is a story about Roman soldiers who lost a battle and they became so angry at the gods that they began to shoot arrows up into the air to kill them. Of course, gravity eventually brought the arrows down killing many of the soldiers. Bitterness is an inward killer.

Psychologist Dr. Theodore Baldick stated that 90 percent of depressed people suffer from spiritual problems.[7] They have used their emotions up in anger and bitterness. As people age, they cannot replenish their emotional energy like when they were younger.

Depression is a depletion of emotional energy and often begins to set in when a person is in their mid-to-late 30s.[8]

One of the consequences of bitterness is the loss of the power of our prayer. How do we forgive? Jesus said,

> "Then Peter came and said to Him, "Lord, how often shall my brother sin against me and I forgive him? Up to seven times?" Jesus said to him, "I do not say to you, up to seven times, but up to seventy times seven."
> (Matthew 18:21-22)

Seventy times seven really means to forgive in an unlimited fashion. But we say, "I will forgive them," and then the next day or the next week something happens to remind us of the incident, and we get angry again. This is what Jesus is speaking about. We forgive the person, sometimes for the same sin over and over again. Each time we forgive it takes longer for the anger to return. Then one day, total forgiveness sets in and we no longer hold that sin against the person.[9]

5) Covetousness

There are other sins that silence our prayers and one of them is a coveting heart, often characterized by a lack of generosity. Proverbs 21:13 says, *"He who shuts his ear to the cry of the poor will also cry himself and not be answered."* Proverbs 11:25 speaks to this in a more positive way. *"A generous man will prosper; he who refreshes others will himself be refreshed." (NIV)* As believers we should be moved to practice grace. Grace is God's undeserved generosity to us. It is said, "We are never more like God than when we give."

6) Wrong motives

In James 4:3 we read, *"You ask and do not receive, because you ask with wrong motives, so that you may spend it on your pleasures."* The only right motive for prayer is to bring glory to God. What is your motive? Here is a test—do you get a little angry when God does not answer your prayer the way you want? If you get upset with God over your request being denied then your request is more important to you than your relationship with God.

7) An indifference to God's Word

"He who turns away his ear from listening to the law, even his prayer is an abomination." (Proverbs 28:9) It is important in our relationship to be anxious to hear from God and apply what we hear. After all, how are we going to find out God's will and pray for it if we do not hear from Him.

In summary, sin will keep our prayers from a *yes* answer. We cannot assume we are clean; we must examine our lives. What can we do?

THE BLESSINGS THAT WE FIND

"If we confess our sins, He is faithful and righteous to forgive us our sins and to cleanse us from all unrighteousness." (I John 1:9)

If we ask God, we can and will be forgiven. There are two key words in this passage. The first is confess which means *to agree with*. We are agreeing with God that there is sin in our lives and we need forgiveness and restoration. It does not mean that we merely ask forgiveness while we keep repeating the same sins. Forgiveness always has an aspect of repentance. Repentance means to turn around and to go a different direction. We can't ask God to forgive us of all we have become only to remain as we are.

The second key word is forgive. There is total forgiveness based on the cross; Jesus paid for all your sins. The word forgive is mentioned in a different way in Matthew 8:15 when Peter's mother-in-law was healed. It says the fever *forgave* (or left) her. When we confess, our sin leaves us. Jeremiah 31:34 says, *"...for I will forgive their iniquity, and their sin I will remember no more."*

Right now you can experience one of God's greatest gifts—forgiveness. I invite you to pray this prayer asking Him to cleanse you.

"Lord, I want to be cleansed. I want my sin forgiven. I want it to leave me. I confess my sin of _____ and I ask You to forgive me as I turn from this awful thing in my life. I lay my sin at the foot of the cross of Christ. If there is anyone I have wronged, please reveal it to me and I will make it right. In Jesus' name, Amen."

Desire: Crying Out to God's Heart

CHAPTER 5

DESIRE: CRYING OUT TO GOD'S HEART

It's a Wonderful Life" is one of my favorite movies. It was made in 1946, but has grown in popularity again during the past several years. I believe one of the reasons it has such a following is because everyone wants their life to count for something. The film is set in a small town in New York State. The main character is George Bailey who has a dream of getting out of his hometown, Bedford Falls. He wants to travel the world and "really be somebody."

However, circumstances keep George in Bedford Falls. He marries, has children and helps everyone in his hometown. His Uncle Billy loses $8,000 (a large amount of money at that time) from their business, the Bailey Building and Loan. As bank president, George will be held accountable for the money. One scene in the movie takes place in "Martini's Bar." George is desperate. Fear is written all over his face—scandal, bankruptcy and prison are facing him. Sitting in the bar, he quietly prays, *"Father in Heaven, I'm not a praying man, but if you are up there and you can hear me, show me the way...*" [1] George Bailey's prayer was one of passion and desire as he cried out in desperation to God.

Do your prayers display a desperation and passion? I am reminded of the little boy whose family was sitting around the dinner table ready to say the blessing. The little boy turned to his dad and said, "Dad, it's my turn to talk to the plates tonight." I think we can all identify with this little boy because most of us have been guilty of sending token prayers to God.

One of the reasons God waits to answer our prayers is because He is testing our true desires. We want dad to receive Christ, but how often do we passionately pray for him? We want a sister to be healed, but how often do we pray or fast for this to happen? If our prayers lack passion, then passion may be the missing ingredient for us to have *yes* answers to our prayers.

In James 5, we find a passage concerning healing. There are many passages in Scripture where someone is healed, but this is the only prescriptive passage for healing in the New Testament.

> "Is anyone among you suffering? Then he must pray. Is anyone cheerful? He is to sing praises. Is anyone among you sick? Then he must call for the elders of the church and they are to pray over him, anointing him with oil in the name of the Lord; and the prayer offered in faith will restore the one who is sick, and the Lord will raise him up, and if he has committed sins, they will be forgiven him. Therefore, confess your sins to one another, and pray for one another so that you may be healed. The effective prayer of a righteous man can accomplish much". (James 5:13-16)

THE PRINCIPLE

There are three areas of suffering, the first being emotional suffering. The Greek word for suffering in verse 13 describes calamity. We go through adversity and trials in life. That is why Jesus admonishes us to be cheerful, that is to have joy in the midst of emotional turmoil. Joy and happiness are very different things. Happiness depends upon things happening or happenstance, but joy is determined by our relationship with God. **Joy comes from the inside out; not the outside in.**

Second, when James asks the question in verse 14, *"Are any of you sick?"* he is referring to physical illness. He then prescribes what we are to do. We are to call for the elders of the church, anoint with oil and pray. I believe the oil to be a symbol of the Holy Spirit and it is not the oil, but the prayer that leads to healing. The third type of suffering is brought on by sin, *"...and if he has committed sins, they will be forgiven him."* The key to the passage is in the next few words. *"The effective prayer of a righteous man can accomplish much."* What does this mean? The righteous man is easy enough to identify. It is a person who is right with God but what about the effective prayer—what makes it effective?

In the original Greek language, the word effective comes from a word meaning *energy* and often refers to passion or heart. In some translations it means *fervency.* A man is pictured crying out to God in desperation. There are many examples of this type of prayer in Scripture. This passage gives us a good example; *"Elijah was a man with a nature like ours, and he prayed earnestly that it would not rain, and it did not rain on the earth for three years and six months." (James 5:17)*

This verse refers back to I Kings and the story of the prophet

Elijah. Elijah knew the nation that did not follow the Lord would not be blessed. He prayed with earnest fervor and passion that it would not rain in Israel and, for the next three and a half years, Israel experienced severe drought; there was no rain. The Bible tells us: *"Call to Me and I will answer you, and I will tell you great and mighty things, which you do not know." (Jeremiah 33:3)* The word call means the same as the Old Testament Hebrew word *cry*.

Scripture also says:

> "Evening and morning and at noon, I will complain and murmur, and He will hear my voice." (Psalm 55:17)

> "In my distress I called upon the LORD, and cried to my God for help; He heard my voice out of His temple, and my cry for help before Him came into His ears." (Psalm 18:6)

One of my favorite examples in the Old Testament is found in the story of the Exodus.

> "Now it came about in the course of those many days that the king of Egypt died. And the sons of Israel sighed because of the bondage, and they cried out; and their cry for help because of their bondage rose up to God. So God heard their groaning; and God remembered His covenant with Abraham, Isaac, and Jacob. God saw the sons of Israel, and God took notice of them." (Exodus 2:23-25)

As God called Moses to the task of rescuing His people, He said,

> "I have surely seen the affliction of My people who are in Egypt, and have given heed to their cry because of their taskmasters, for I am aware of their sufferings.

> So I have come down to deliver them from the power
> of the Egyptians, and to bring them up from that land
> to a good and spacious land, to a land flowing with
> milk and honey, to the place of the Canaanite and
> the Hittite and the Amorite and the Perizzite and the
> Hivite and the Jebusite." (Exodus 3:7, 8)

God placed the Israelites under Egyptian bondage and they cried out for help. There is something in a heartfelt cry that gets God's attention: a crying out in shameless humility—not caring what others think. A passionate, humble heart leads to answered prayer. God illustrates this in human relationships. If our house is on fire, we don't calmly walk through the house informing our family to pack up and make their way to the door. We would behave with alarming passion and perhaps panic. Charles Spurgeon said, *"He who prays without fervency does not pray at all."* [2]

THE PURPOSE

Why does a blessing come to those who cry out to God? First and foremost it's because of the **humility** on their part. Psalm 9:12 says, *"(God) does not forget the cry of the humble."* James 5:6 states, *"God gives grace to the humble."* Every answer to prayer is an act of God's grace.

When a person receives Christ, he is crying out to God for help (Romans 10:13). He recognizes that he cannot save himself. What would happen if a person realized his sinfulness and sent up a token prayer to God—"Lord I can do this salvation thing on my own, but bless my efforts as I go." Certainly we know people who have prayed this way. In Romans 1 it says,

"...because that which is known about God is evident within them; for God made it evident to them. For since the creation of the world His invisible attributes, His eternal power and divine nature, have been clearly seen, being understood through what has been made, so that they are without excuse. For even though they knew God, they did not honor Him as God or give thanks, but they became futile in their speculations, and their foolish heart was darkened." (Romans 1:19-21)

Chapters 1-3 of Romans teach us that everyone is lost without Christ. Chapter 1 says the heathen (those who have never heard the gospel) are lost. God made Himself evident in nature and in people's hearts, therefore they are accountable. Chapter 2 says we find the moralist is lost and Chapter 3 tells us the religious person is lost without Christ. It may be argued that the later two groups are lost because they are stealing the glory (honor) of God.

The moralist says, "I can work my way to favor with God," and feels he does not have to give God glory for what Jesus did on the cross. He believes he can give himself the glory by earning his own salvation. The religious person thinks that he is pleasing God by his religious activity. He will not trust Christ alone to save him. He adds works to Christ; thus, trying to share in the glory of God.

When we send up a less than heartfelt prayer to God, in essence we say the issue is almost covered; "I really don't need your help, but I don't want to leave you out." Or we are saying "God I cannot do it alone, I need your help to bless my efforts but I will share in your glory."

The heartfelt cry of the believer says, "Lord I am at a loss. I cannot do this. I am crying out to You for help because only You can make this happen." When God says *yes* to your passionate prayer,

He gets all the glory and you get His grace.

A second reason for fervent praying is that it **builds our faith**. It gives us courage. There is something encouraging about listening to our own voice that confirms our faith. Author and teacher, Bill Gothard said, *"As we call aloud, we can more easily recognize our heart's condition before God. Hearing our own spoken words, we quickly detect any lack of fervency, humility or reverence. Listening to ourselves, we are forced to examine our hearts."* [3]

Another reason for heartfelt crying out to God is it **reveals our heart**. We often do not know the intensity of our own feelings until we voice them. In the story of blind Bartimaeus in Mark 10, we find a blind man on the side of the road. As Jesus walked by, Bartimaeus began to follow, crying out, *"Oh, son of David, have mercy on me."* Jesus' disciples rebuked him, *"Don't bother the master..."* The Bible tells us that *"...he cried all the more."* He was not worried about what others would think. As Bartimaeus spoke it gave him courage and affirmed the deepest need of his heart—he wanted to see. Have you found yourself suppressing the urge to cry out to God and pour out your heart to Him?

THE PARTICULARS

In James 5, we find several things that are worth crying out for, including sickness and suffering. What are some of the things for which you and I need to cry out? We are invited to cry out in prayer for our trials and sufferings. *"Then they cried out to the LORD in their trouble; He delivered them out of their distresses."* *(Psalm 107:6)*

Previously I shared with you the story of my healing from diabetes. On that eventful evening as I praised God and prayed fervently about several matters, I did not cry out to God for healing but I nevertheless cried out to Him. As God heard my prayers for others, He laid it on my heart to pray for myself. I did—and He answered.

Another way we want to apply passionate prayer is when we are in desperation for others. Several years ago I preached a week-long revival. The first night a weeping man came forward during the invitation. I learned that he had only been a Christian for a few years. He had raised his daughter in an unchurched home and after he became a Christian his daughter, Tammy, would not listen to what he had to say. His earlier life had taught her that God was not important. The die was cast and it would seem that he had been saved too late to save his daughter. He further shared with me that Tammy was now 18 and addicted to drugs. She had left home and he had not seen her for weeks. This man was desperate. He was at the end of this rope and was crying out for God's help.

God worked a miracle later in that week. After the message on Thursday night, I extended the invitation for people to come and receive Christ. The first person down the aisle was a dark-haired young lady. As she began walking down the aisle, I had to resist the temptation to meet her and help her. Whether it was from drugs or conviction, she moved slowly and weakly toward me. When she reached the front of the church, she held out her hand and said tearfully, "I want to receive Christ." Her name was Tammy and she was the daughter of the man who had cried out to God earlier that week. God answers the cries of His people.

Not only should we cry out for others, but also for ourselves. When we planted a church in Atlanta, we found ourselves reaching many unchurched people. Often the newer people were not familiar with church etiquette. It was not unusual for someone to walk in during church service and to look around for relatives or friends, so I was not alarmed when a man walked in near the end of my message and stood in the back. I was immersed in the message and forgot about him. As I gave the invitation to come forward and make a decision for Christ several people came forward. While speaking to one young lady, I noticed the next person in line—the man who came in late. He was wearing a tank-top shirt, gym shorts and sandals and had a very stern look on his face. This made me nervous because there had been recent episodes around the city where church services were disrupted and in fact, a pastor friend of mine had been shot and killed in his study. This man reached out to shake my hand and he began to cry. He asked, "Is there room at the cross for me?" As it turns out, this man was desperate. He did not know where to turn. That particular morning he had cried out to God for help. On his way to breakfast, he saw our church sign with the title of the message "Help for Hurting People." As he pulled into the restaurant parking lot, he prayed, "God, I am that hurting person. Maybe this is the answer to my prayer." He turned his car around, drove to the church and walked through the door in time to hear the end of the message. Praise God for heartfelt prayer!

Perhaps no encounter was more astonishing and touching to me than the story of Susan. One Monday evening I was training two of my church members in how to share their faith. Our assignment that evening was to go on door-to-door visitation. For awhile, we found no one at home. Then I knocked on a door and a lady answered. We introduced ourselves and upon hearing our purpose, she looked at us hatefully and said, "How dare you knock on my door. Everyone around here who wants religion, has religion. No one is interested in what you have to say." Her response took me aback, especially having two people with me who had never shared their faith.

Well, I knew this could not stop us because God had us there for a reason. A few doors down, I saw a car in the driveway and figuring someone was probably home, I knocked on the door and a young lady answered. I told her who we were and where we were from. Shocked, she looked like she had seen a ghost. She introduced herself as Susan and asked us to come in.

After we shared the gospel presentation, she told us her story. She suffered from cystic fibrosis and she was not expected to live past the age of 25. She had just celebrated her 25th birthday by getting drunk and partying. That morning she awoke depressed and hung over. Though she rarely skipped work, she decided to stay home. She could not recall ever having any deep spiritual thoughts, but her mood that day became introspective as she found herself thinking about life, eternity and God. She suddenly realized all her efforts had changed nothing and her life was empty. She cried out, "God, if you are real, please send someone to my house to speak to me about You today." We then understood her reaction when she first saw us at the door. A few months later she made a decision for Christ. Praise the Lord for another answer for someone who had cried out to God.

In Scripture we find a great example of heartfelt prayer. David, after committing the sin of adultery and conspiring to murder, became greatly convicted. He cried out in prayer.

> "Be gracious to me, O God, according to Your lovingkindness; according to the greatness of Your

compassion blot out my transgressions. Wash me thoroughly from my iniquity and cleanse me from my sin. For I know my transgressions, and my sin is ever before me. Against You, You only, I have sinned and done what is evil in Your sight, so that You are justified when You speak and blameless when You judge". (Psalm 51:1-4)

"Hide Your face from my sins and blot out all my iniquities. Create in me a clean heart, O God, and renew a steadfast spirit within me. Do not cast me away from Your presence and do not take Your Holy Spirit from me. Restore to me the joy of Your salvation and sustain me with a willing spirit. Then I will teach transgressors Your ways, and sinners will be converted to You." (Psalm 51:9-13)

James 5:15 says, "...and the prayer offered in faith will restore the one who is sick, and the Lord will raise him up, and if he has committed sins, they will be forgiven him."

When we sin against the Lord, our fellowship is broken. We no longer have the joy of salvation, the peace of God in our hearts (Philippians 4:7) or freedom from guilt. What better reason do we have to cry out to God?

Finally, let me focus on the need to cry out for spiritual power. David prayed "On the day I called, You answered me; You made me bold with strength in my soul." (Psalm 138:3)

Paul cried out to God for the church at Ephesus to be filled with spiritual power.

"For this reason I bow my knees before the Father, from whom every family in heaven and on earth derives its name, that He would grant you, according to the riches of His glory, to be strengthened with power through His Spirit in the inner man, so that Christ may dwell in your hearts through faith; and that you, being rooted and grounded in love, may be able to comprehend with all the saints what is the breadth and length and height and depth, and to know the love of Christ which surpasses knowledge, that you may be filled up to all the fullness of God." (Ephesians 3:14-19)

There was a story in the Dallas Morning News that illustrated the power of prayer. Sherman Jackson told of riding to church on a Sunday morning with his seven-year-old daughter in the front seat of his car. He stopped at a convenience store and a man knocked on his window. Sherman rolled down the window and asked, "Can I help you?" The man explained that his car had stalled down the road and wondered if Sherman could give him a ride back to his car and help him "jump" it. After chastising himself for selfishly thinking about being late to church, Sherman replied, "Sure, I'll help you." He put his daughter in the back seat and the man got into the front seat beside Sherman. After traveling only a short way the passenger pulled out a gun and demanded all of Sherman's money. Sherman reached into his pocket and said, "Here, take it all. It's all I have." The man replied, "I don't believe you." Sherman was a Gideon and had several Gideon Bibles in his car. He had a practice of placing a dollar bill inside each Bible with the end of the bill protruding a little as he would hand out the Bibles. The man saw the Bibles and became incensed. "You've been lying to me." In desperation, Sherman cried out to God—"I pray right now that you would bless my life, help this man, and deliver me from this evil." The man did not know what to think. Sherman stopped the car and made a U-turn. "What are you doing?" the man asked. Sherman replied, "I'm taking you back to the convenience store." The man cocked the gun and stuck it against Sherman's chest. He said, "I'm going to kill you!" Sherman replied, "You can't touch me unless God wants you to touch me." Sherman pulled off the road, stopped the car and said, "I want to tell you about Jesus." The man put down his gun and began to cry as Sherman shared Christ with him.

Some doubted this story until a few weeks later when a man by the name of Mike was arrested for robbery. He had robbed 15 people the way he attempted to rob Sherman. God answered Sherman's desperate prayer with spiritual power.[4]

Speaking of power, look at the results of heartfelt, passionate prayer. This is the promise from God... *"The effective (fervent) prayer of a righteous man accomplishes much." (James 5:16)*

Perhaps you do not receive enough *yes* answers because you are not crying out to God. **Your cries are heard in heaven and God desires to answer as you humble yourself before Him and give Him glory.** I invite you to join me in discovering the great things God will do when you cry out to Him.

This brings me to the final key in getting God to say *yes*. When you have the desire, the determination will follow.

Determination:
Persistence
Before God's
Throne

CHAPTER 6

DETERMINATION: PERSISTENCE BEFORE GOD'S THRONE

What do these children's prayers have in common?

"Dear God…thank you for my baby brother, but what I prayed for was a puppy."

"Dear God…please send me a pony. I never asked for anything before. You can look it up."

"Dear God…I bet it is hard for you to love all the people in the world. There are only four people in our family and I can't do it."

"Dear God…if you watch me in church this Sunday, I'll show you my new shoes."

"Dear God…maybe Cain and Abel would not kill each other so much if they had their own rooms. It works with my brother."

These prayers all expect God to hear and to answer. Perhaps you have been praying for a lost loved one for 20 or 30 years or you have been asking God for a new job for the past six months. Maybe your marriage is in trouble and you feel the more you pray, the worse it gets.

How long should we pray for a situation? Why isn't God

answering more quickly? Do we have to pester God until He answers? Sometimes, we feel like the little boy upstairs in bed who called down to his dad asking for a glass of water. His dad, knowing the boy was fighting sleep, refused the request. Finally, after several attempts, his dad said, "Son, if you do not be quiet and go to sleep, I am going to come up there and spank you." After a short period of silence, the little boy replied, "Dad when you come up to spank me, would you bring me a glass of water?"

I have stated that there are three possible answers to prayer—*yes, no,* and *wait.* Let's look more closely at why God would have us *wait.*

As Jesus was speaking about His second coming, He taught the disciples a lesson in perseverance or persistence in prayer.

> "Now He was telling them a parable to show that at all times they ought to pray and not to lose heart, saying, "In a certain city there was a judge who did not fear God and did not respect man. There was a widow in that city, and she kept coming to him, saying, 'Give me legal protection from my opponent.' For a while he was unwilling; but afterward he said to himself, 'Even though I do not fear God nor respect man, yet because this widow bothers me, I will give her legal protection, otherwise by continually coming she will wear me out.'" And the Lord said, "Hear what the unrighteous judge said; now, will not God bring about justice for His elect who cry to Him day and night, and will He delay long over them? I tell you that He will bring about justice for them quickly. However, when the Son of Man comes, will He find faith on the earth?" (Luke 18:1-8)

Reading these verses one might think that God is reluctant to answer our prayers and that we do have to pester God. Since this is a parable and a parable always has one main point, let's explore that point.

THE EXPLANATION OF THE PARABLE

In verse one, we learn to keep on praying—never giving up on our prayers. This verse begins by telling us that we need to pray at all times inferring the need for watchfulness. It brings to mind an on-duty police officer, constantly on the lookout. We are to be looking for opportunities to pray and to have our prayers answered.

Then verse one tells us not to lose heart, reflecting the phrase used in Galatians 6:9 where it says, *"Let us not lose heart in doing good; for in due time we will reap, if we do not grow weary."* Looking at this verse, we find we are given the option to pray or to faint (give up).

Verse 2 begins a parable about an unjust judge who gets annoyed by one woman's persistence for justice. This woman stops him and is very tenacious in her request. He is busy as he has several cases to judge before the day is done. She needs legal protection from an opponent and she begins to beg him to help her. Finally, he says, *"Even though I do not fear God nor respect man yet because this widow bothers me, I will give her legal protection, otherwise by continually coming she will wear me out."*

As we look at the story about an ungodly judge I'd like to point out that Jesus taught in two different ways with His parables: one is a teaching by comparison, where we compare God to something else; the other way is by contrast. For example, when Jesus said… *"If a man gives a child a fish, do you think God is going to give you a stone?"*—this is teaching by contrast. So this parable does not teach that God is unjust, stubborn and uncaring. Rather, it is contrasting God with this judge.

The lesson is that if an unrighteous judge will give you what you need, how much more (in contrast) will your heavenly Father meet your needs?

We find the thrust of the parable in verse 8. *"I tell you that He will bring about justice for them quickly. However, when the Son of Man comes, will He find faith on the earth?"*

In Luke 17, Jesus is speaking about His second coming. He is telling them He is coming again. However, we will have to wait for the time to be right. The time, the season, the people, the government will all come together. When the time is right in God's plan, He will return.

Just like we are to wait for God's timing for Jesus to return and His orchestration of the end-times, we are also to wait for God to orchestrate the circumstances (the time, season and people) to answer our prayers. I remind you of the reasons why God might wait to answer our prayers: something bigger is in the overall plan of God; something better is in the overall plan; something is binding the overall plan of God. (See Chapter 3.) In short, God has a plan and He works all people, places and circumstances together to bring about the answer to prayer. What can we do? Scripture teaches, *"Ask, and it will be given to you; seek, and you will find; knock, and it will be opened to you."* (Matthew 7:7) Keep on knocking!

Is there a time when we should cease to knock?

One of my theology professors in college taught that we should pray about something one time and after that simply thank God for answering the prayer. While I do not completely agree with this approach, I do think that there is a time to stop asking and to start thanking God. When we have a lasting peace in our hearts that our prayer is as good as answered, it is time to rejoice and give thanks. Colossians 3:15 says, *"Let the peace of Christ rule in your hearts, to which indeed you were called in one body; and be thankful."* In the original language, it says that peace is to act like an umpire in our hearts and when we have peace, we are to give thanks. Until we have the peace that God will, and in a sense has answered that prayer, we need to keep on knocking.

THE APPLICATION TO OUR PRAYERS

If God is all powerful then why can't He pull all the conditions and circumstances together more quickly? Why does He make us wait?

While we are waiting, God wants to do some really great things in our lives. First, as we are persistent in our praying, our attention on God is more focused. If all our prayers are answered, it will actually be destructive to our lives. As James Dobson infers, spoiling a child comes not just from giving the child everything he wants, but more importantly giving him what he wants when he wants it.[1] If we receive everything we pray for quickly, then we become spoiled. God will be little more than a genie in a lamp or a vending machine. Every time we want something, we pop in a prayer and out would come the answer. There would be no getting to know God or drawing closer to Him.

When Moses went up on Mt. Sinai for forty days to receive the law there is no question that God could have given him the tablets the first day. However, it says in Exodus 34 that when Moses came down, his face was shining like the face of God. He had to place a veil over his face because the rest of the people could not look upon him. Moses got close to God while He was waiting.

A second reason we are kept waiting is because persistence declares and intensifies our desire for the prayer request. I refer back to the example of a child: when you do not give to your child immediately, it tests how much they want something. When our children were young, starting around October they would begin to drop hints about what they wanted for Christmas. Often the desire would change from week to week depending on the latest television commercial. However, when they really locked on to what they wanted, we never heard the end of it. By the time Christmas arrived, we were almost willing to give them their present early so we could have a little peace. Without question, they appreciated and enjoyed the gifts more, having waited.

A third reason for waiting is that it helps build patience and endurance in our lives. Hebrews 10:36 says, *"For you have need of endurance, so that when you have done the will of God, you may receive what was promised."* After we do God's will, we sometimes must wait to receive whatever God has promised. The entire eleventh chapter of Hebrews concerns enduring faith. Hebrews 12:1-3 concludes this "hall of faith" passage by giving the example of Jesus who endured the cross for us. Without patience and endurance there are many character traits in our lives that will not become developed. Without patience we will not endure to receive answers to prayer that God wants in our lives.

In the 1960s a study was done by psychologist, Dr. Daniel Goleman. The study involved experiments concerning delayed gratification among four year olds. Dr. Goleman would enter a preschool class and give each child a marshmallow. He told the children that he was going to leave the room and if they waited until he returned to eat their marshmallow, they would be given another one as a prize. He left the room for twenty minutes and continued to watch by camera. Several of the children looked at the marshmallow and smelled it, but did not eat it. Others popped it into their mouths right way. Still others waited several minutes until they lost patience and finally ate the marshmallow. Thirty years later, hundreds of those who had been involved in the experiment were interviewed. The ones who waited to eat the marshmallow and received another marshmallow as a reward, were more disciplined and showed more mature decisions in their lives than their counterparts.[2] Waiting builds patience and patience builds character.

> "And not only this, but we also exult in our tribulations, knowing that tribulation brings about perseverance; and perseverance, proven character; and proven character, hope; and hope does not disappoint, because the love of God has been poured out within our hearts through the Holy Spirit who was given to us." (Romans 5:3-5)

A fourth reason for patient, persistent praying is because of spiritual warfare.

In Daniel 10 we read,

> "But I heard the sound of his words; and as soon as I heard the sound of his words, I fell into a deep sleep on my face, with my face to the ground. Then behold, a hand touched me and set me trembling on my hands and knees. He said to me, "O Daniel, man of high esteem, understand the words that I am about to tell you and stand upright, for I have now been sent to you "And when he had spoken this word to me, I stood up trembling. Then he said to me, "Do not be

afraid, Daniel, for from the first day that you set your
heart on understanding this and on humbling yourself
before your God, your words were heard, and I have
come in response to your words. But the prince of the
kingdom of Persia was withstanding me for twenty-
one days; then behold, Michael, one of the chief
princes, came to help me, for I had been left there with
the kings of Persia." (Daniel 10:9-13)

In this passage, the prophet Daniel had a vision of the future
but he was unsure of the interpretation. He began to pray to the
Lord to give him the answer. Spiritual opposition was strong—the
prince of Persia (a demon) was sent to delay the answer to prayer.
The demon is pictured as being so powerful that God sent the
Archangel Michael to assist the angel who was speaking to Daniel.
This story offers a glimpse of what goes on behind the scenes.
Perhaps you have been backstage at a play or attended a meeting
in the boardroom of a major business—you get a glimpse of what
goes on behind the play or business.

My daughter, Lauren is a country music fan and I mentioned
this to a friend of mine who lives in Tennessee. He told me that
he could get us backstage passes to the Grand Ole Opry when we
were in Nashville and we gratefully accepted his offer.

The next time we were in Nashville we went "country." The
music stars were very friendly and Lauren was able to get her picture taken with some of the performers. We even sat behind the
band on stage looking out on the rest of the audience.

Just like we received a glimpse of the backstage of the Opry,
God is giving us a small glimpse of behind the scenes of prayer.
God draws back the curtain and we see the spiritual warfare.
Daniel prayed for 21 days for the same thing until the angel was

able to get him an answer. What would have happened if Daniel had stopped praying after 15 or 16 days? We will never know, but it would seem that Satan has the power to delay, though not deny, our prayers.

Maybe you are praying for a lost loved one, a prodigal son to return, a job or marriage difficulties. You think the answer will never come and you feel God has abandoned you. Perhaps you are not defeated about a situation, but you no longer pray about it with any fervency. That is another way of saying that you no longer believe God is going to answer your prayers. Maybe behind the scenes of prayer, God is sending the answer even now.

A final reason waiting is necessary is because God is preparing us for the answer. When we pray, God begins to bring together all the people and circumstances involved. Sometimes we are not ready for the answer. In the interim, **God wants to mature us so that we can handle the blessing.**

A common term in ministry is "shooting star." This refers to a young minister who rises quickly in the ministry and seems to be greatly blessed; but sometimes he is not mature enough to handle the success, his pride gets the better of him and he falls. His fall could be in the form of an extra-marital affair or ethical violations, particularly concerning money. Some pastors develop a sense of entitlement, become arrogant and simply stop doing the little things that drew people to them in the beginning. No matter the vocation, any of us can fall prey to pride and temptation. We need time to grow as God prepares us for a blessing.

Often growth comes through trials and part of the trial can be the waiting itself.

"Consider it all joy, my brethren, when you encounter various trials, knowing that the testing of your faith produces endurance. And let endurance have its perfect result, so that you may be perfect and complete, lacking in nothing." (James 1:2-4)

Sometimes we must wait for the answer because God has something different in mind. When I graduated from seminary I wanted to count for God. I had big dreams and visions for my ministry. God blessed my wife and me with the privilege of starting a church near Atlanta. My first vision was to plant the church, construct a building and make it a viable entity. After about two and a half years that mission was accomplished.

Then God gave me another vision of one day pastoring a church with over 2,000 in attendance. The Atlanta church continued to grow, but encountered obstacles along the way. The neighborhood began to transition and many of the members did not want a large church. Sometimes I felt I was taking three steps forward and then two steps back, dragging the church behind me.

After almost nine years of ministry there, God moved my family to our present church in Florida. God has richly blessed and fulfilled His promise. When I began this pastorate, the attendance was around 600 in worship. It now averages over 2,500 in worship and almost 2,000 in small groups. God has been faithful. To God be the glory!

I share this example of waiting because in my early church I did not possess the maturity to handle the enormous task nor the blessing of such a large ministry so God had me wait for His will. God's timing is just as important as God's will. Some of the greatest blessings in my life have come after prayerful waiting.

THE MOTIVATION FOR OUR PERSISTENCE

As we wait, what should we do? First, we need to keep on praying—this is what determination is all about. We need to keep on persevering in prayer until God answers—one way or the other.

> "...yet because this widow bothers me, I will give her legal protection, otherwise by continually coming she will wear me out." (Luke 18:5)

> "Wait for the LORD; be strong and let your heart take courage; yes, wait for the LORD." (Psalm 27:14)

Earlier I shared with you how I came to Christ. Let me elaborate on the story. My parents were married soon after World War II. There was not much teaching on marriage in churches at that time, particularly in the small country church in which my mother was raised. The subject of being unequally yoked with an unbeliever was not a frequent subject in sermons (II Corinthians 6:14). As a Christian, Mom felt that she just wanted to marry a good man which meant to her, one who was honest, hard working, and would treat her well. She found that man in my dad.

Not long after they were married she learned that her new husband was not motivated to go to church and as the children arrived, she became concerned with the situation. There were times when my mom would stop going to church rather than sit alone. There were other times my dad would attend and actually become convicted to come to Christ. However, before he would make a decision something would happen to chase him from church. One Sunday a man actually embarrassed my dad by begging him and coaxing him down the aisle during the invitation while the church stood and watched.

Through the years my mom never stopped praying for Dad's salvation. By the time he was in his early 40s Dad had become comfortable driving us children to Sunday School and waiting in the car. Then one Friday evening as my mom was shopping, my twelve year old brother was sitting in the car with Dad. Barry said, "Hey Dad, my Sunday School teacher said you sure would be proud of me if I got saved." Dad was stunned and simply muttered back, "Son, I'm proud of you no matter what you do." After my brother left the car Dad was alone with his thoughts. Later he told me that he confessed to the Lord, "God, if one of my boys died tonight they would go to hell and it would be my fault." The next Sunday, my dad took our family to church and it was obvious to us that he had taken a new interest in God.

Sometime later I received Christ as my Savior and Lord, keeping my decision quiet and wondering what to do next. Then our church conducted a series of revival meetings. My brother and I went forward during the invitation, openly professing our faith in Christ. Before the first verse of the invitation hymn ended, my dad also came forward to receive Christ. He said that God deeply touched his heart when he saw us respond and he wasn't going to let the devil talk him out of it again! My mom also recommitted her life to Christ. I did not fully understand her tears that night, but today I do. After 20 years of marriage, my mom's prayers were answered.

Why should we keep on praying? Because it is an act of faith. We are saying that through doubt, adversity and tears, we still trust Him. God always keeps His Word—just never give up. What is our ultimate objective in getting God to say *yes*? Is it enough just to receive His blessings? What does He want us to do with these changes in our lives?

SUMMARIZATION OF CHAPTERS 2-6

God wants to answer your prayers because they can make a difference in your life and in the lives of others. You should pray even when you are not sure of the answer. However, all of us want *yes* answers. Let's review the five keys to getting *yes*.

(1) Dependence: Trusting in God's Character

Is your confidence in God or in your own faith? Faith is trusting God for your future, believing in the unseen, and in taking Him at His Word. Faith is not wishful thinking or great desire but it is resting in what God has actually promised. What has God promised to you? Those are the promises He will fulfill.

(2) Direction: Committed to God's Will

In order to receive a *yes* answer, you must know the will of God on a matter and be committed to it. The will of God is not a limitation but an opportunity to see and experience great things. Do you really want something that would take you out of the will of God?

(3) Devotion: Forgiven through God's Grace

Is there any unconfessed sin in your life that would hinder God from answering your prayers? When there is sin in our lives, our

111

fellowship with God is broken and hurt. It's not that God will say *no* to our prayer, rather He will not hear that prayer with an intention to answer. We must confess our sins (I John 1:9) and have a clean heart before God in order to get *yes* answers.

(4) Desire: Crying Out to God's Heart

Is there passion behind your prayers? James 5:16 says, *"...The effective (fervent) prayer of a righteous man can accomplish much."* God holds a special place in His heart for those who pray desperately and passionately. Reveal your heart's desires before God and you will see Him called into action.

(5) Determination: Persistence Before God's Throne

Have you stopped praying just before God sends the answer? You are in spiritual warfare. You not only need fervency in your prayers, but also tenacity. God is testing your desires. He is bringing together the elements and circumstances to answer your prayer. Don't give up!

All of us need effective prayer lives. Your nation needs your prayers. Your family needs your prayers. Surely there are people in your life who are far removed from the Christian experience and you are the only one praying for them. These people need a prayer warrior whose arrows are sharp and effective. You have an opportunity to make a difference—*"That Your (God's) way may be known on the earth, Your (God's) salvation among the nations."* (Psalm 67:2)

THIS PRAYER'S
FOR YOU

CHAPTER 7

THIS PRAYER'S FOR YOU

Everyone wants answers to their prayers. Most of us simply want to live successfully. We want God to bless our family, our professional life, our finances and our health. But our ultimate objective should be sharing in the blessings of God.

Bruce Wilkinson's book entitled, *"The Prayer of Jabez"* was so popular that it became a New York Times best seller. The book was based on a prayer by Jabez in I Chronicles 4:9, 10.

> "Jabez was more honorable than his brothers, and his mother named him Jabez saying, "Because I bore him with pain." Now Jabez called on the God of Israel, saying, "Oh that You would bless me indeed and enlarge my border, and that Your hand might be with me, and that You would keep me from harm that it may not pain me!" And God granted him what he requested."

Many have criticized Wilkinson's book for a perceived misuse of the prayer. They reasoned that it was a self-centered prayer and never meant to be used by anyone but Jabez himself. In other words, it was descriptive of what he prayed, but not prescriptive of what we should pray.

However, God never rebuked Jabez for his prayer. He actually answered the prayer. Although it is not prescriptive in context, there is nothing written that says what worked for Jabez will not work for you. I have prayed this prayer on many occasions and I believe God has answered it.

What falls short in this prayer is our ultimate objective as a believer—to be a blessing to others. The prayer of Jabez took the Christian world by storm because it was a prayer for personal success. But success is not enough. "Success is when I add value to myself. Significance is when I add value to others."[1]

> "You and I live in an age when only a rare minority of individuals desire to spend their lives in pursuit of objectives which are bigger than they are. In our age, for most people, when they die it will be as though they never lived." [2] Rusty Rustenbach, Giving Yourself Away

This quote came to mind when my first grandchild was born. When I saw my son and grandson together for the first time I was reminded that successful parenting means raising children to follow the Lord, but significant parenting means raising generations of children to follow the Lord. Success is God blessing what you are responsible for in your life and significance occurs when there is a multiplication of your efforts which positively affects the lives of others.

Psalm 67, written by an unknown author, reminds me of the prayer of Jabez. It too is a prayer for personal success, but goes a giant step further.

"God be gracious to us and bless us, and cause His face to shine upon us— Selah. That Your way may be known on the earth, Your salvation among all nations. Let the peoples praise You, O God; Let all the peoples praise You. Let the nations be glad and sing for joy; for You will judge the peoples with uprightness and guide the nations on the earth. Selah. Let the peoples praise You, O God; let all the peoples praise You. The earth has yielded its produce; God, our God, blesses us. God blesses us, that all the ends of the earth may fear Him". (Psalm 67:1-7)

THE REQUESTS

The psalmist began the passage with the name Elohim (God), calling on Him to do something great in his life and in the nation of Israel. He used the name for God's greatness. It is the name of the God of creation, the One who is majestic, the One who can do all things—as in Genesis 1:1 where it says, *"In the beginning God created the heavens and the earth."* By merely calling Elohim, the Psalmist performed an act of worship. This is typical of Old Testament prayers. As he read the first five books of the Bible, he remembered all that God had done for his people. He thought about the mighty acts of creation, the exodus, the miracles, and he wanted God to do something great again.

What did he want God to do? Here we find a three-fold prayer. First, he prayed that the Lord would show His grace. *"God be gracious to us..."* Grace has been defined as "God's unmerited or undeserved favor." Simply put, it's the generosity of God toward us. Scripture implies that all we have is from God's generous heart. A financial blessing is an act of God's grace; a healing of the physical body is an act of God's grace; knowledge of Scripture is an act of God's grace as are spiritual gifts or talents.

When we think of grace, we first think of our salvation. Ephesians 2:8, 9 says, *"For by grace you have been saved through faith; and that not of yourselves, it is the gift of God; not as a result of the works, so that no one may boast."* We can do nothing to save ourselves. Works cannot save us. We must humbly surrender to God and to what Christ did on the cross, and ask Him to come into our hearts so we may receive the gift of salvation. Like salvation, the blessings for the Christian are from God's grace. The psalmist recognizes that everything we have comes from God and we can do nothing but humbly surrender and ask Him to give us His daily grace.

The second request is that God will *"bless us."* As I think of this word bless, I am drawn back to the beatitudes of Matthew 5:1-12. There Jesus says that the poor in spirit, those who mourn, those who are meek and pure in heart are blessed. This word blessed comes from the concept of God's hand being upon your life which results in happiness or joy in your heart. While grace comes from the heart of God, blessings come from the hand of God. In order to be blessed we must be in a place where God will bless us. The fourth verse of Psalm 67 says, *"...and guide the nations on the earth."* We need to be in God's path of blessing to fully experience His hand upon our life. I'm not saying that our blessings are earned, but rather we need to be in the place God wants us to be (guided by His will) when the blessings arrive in our lives. You have heard the expression, "He was at the right place at the right time," so we need to be at the right place at the right time by following the will of God. He would not be wise to bless us when we are living a life apart from Him; it would only encourage disobedience.

The final request in this Psalm has to do with seeking the face of God and His divine presence in our lives. He writes, *"...and cause His face to shine upon us."* According to the Scriptures, no one has ever seen the face of God. In the book of Exodus, the Bible says that Moses had to look upon the back of God because no one could look upon the face of God and live.

II Chronicles 7:14 says, *"...and My people who are called by My name humble themselves and pray and seek My face and turn from their wicked ways, then I will hear from heaven, will forgive their sin and will heal their land."* Notice it says we are to seek His face which represents the presence and glory of God and not His hand which represents the blessings of God.

Remember Moses coming down from Mt. Sinai—the Bible says his face was shining so bright that the people of Israel could not look upon him. God's presence will illuminate our lives. When our lives are shining with the presence of God, several things happen: we will sense His presence; He will give us a powerful walk of faith; others will sense something different in us; and we have God's favor. In Scripture when God's face was turned toward you, it was a picture of God's blessings and favor. When God's face was turned away it was a symbol of God's judgment as He withdrew His favor.

How do we get God's favor?—by spending time in His presence. When Moses' face was shining, it was the effect of having spent time with God. The prayer of Psalm 67 cannot be fulfilled by merely praying the prayer—it must be practiced. We practice it by walking with God which means that we spend time in God's Word and obey it. A good rule of thumb for our walk with God is:

worship in church weekly; meet with Him daily; pray to Him continuously; and share your faith regularly.

Worship is a time when we give glory to God as a church body. When someone comes to you to thank you for how you have been inspirational in their lives, it is a wonderful compliment. However, when a large group of people come together and give you a standing ovation for your accomplishments, it can be an unforgettable experience. Personally thanking God is like thanking another person. Corporate worship as a church body is the standing ovation that we give to God. When we do not worship God as a church, He does not receive the honor He is due. **When we do not attend worship, we do not have the full experience of having His face shine upon us.**

You and I need a daily time alone with God. I would encourage you to purchase a journal so you can record how God is speaking to you each day. Writing about your daily quiet time will go far beyond mere reading. I use and recommend "The Spiritual Journal" written by Dr. Billie Hanks, Jr. and Billy Beacham. I have found that the one thing separating those who sense God's heart, hand and face upon them each day from those who do not is their daily quiet time with God. In order to sense God's presence we need to pray consistently. The more answers we receive in prayer, the more we pray. The more we pray, the closer we feel to God.

We need to share our faith regularly. It is vital that we show outwardly what God is working inwardly. When we witness for Christ, we become His mouthpiece, His conduit to others and this act of witnessing makes God feel closer to us. God's favor is upon us when we act on His Word. Jesus taught us, at the close of his ministry, to go and share the gospel.

"Go therefore and make disciples of all the nations,
baptizing them in the name of the Father and the Son
and the Holy Spirit, teaching them to observe all that
I commanded you; and lo, I am with you always, even
to the end of the age." (Matthew 28:19, 20)

This brings me to the why behind the prayer.

THE RESULTS

Psalm 67 is my prayer for you because there are three results of
this prayer that lead to significance.

First, "...*that Your way may be known on the earth, Your salvation among all nations.*"(Verse 2) There were many reasons why
God chose a people in the Old Testament. For one, the Israelites
were chosen to write the Scriptures and preserve them. They were
also chosen to be a witness to the Gentile nations. The Jews were
to live in victory so that the people of other nations would come to
God, repent and follow Him. The Psalmist's request was that God
would be gracious, bless and shine His face upon His people, then
nations would see it and want to know their God.

In Psalm 67:2 the word *way* refers to the principles and rules by
which God governs man.[3] Through our witness, the people of the
world should recognize what is right and fair. The word salvation
in Christian application refers to a person coming to know Christ
as Savior and Lord. The ultimate objective for seeking answers to
our prayers is so the non-believer will see how God is working in
our lives and want what we have. In Luke 19:10, Jesus said, "*For the
Son of Man has come to seek and to save that which was lost.*"

Most of our prayers are more self-centered rather than God-
centered and others-centered. This is where I see the prayer of

Jabez and many of our personal prayers fall short. We often have tunnel vision. We experience many challenges in life and we want to know that God is with us. A way that we know God is there for us and others is through answered prayer.

Suppose there were two ladies in your church who had physical difficulties. Both sought and prayed for healing; one was healed, the other was not. The one who was healed gave glory to God and often testified of her blessing from God. The second lady was not healed, yet she rejoiced that her friend had been touched by God. The lady who was not healed was an inspiration to those around her. Her attitude was godly. In her obvious pain, she was actually an encouragement to others. Her unchurched friends took notice of how she was victorious in life in spite of her illness. Which of these ladies would be a greater testimony to the world?

I know some would argue that the healed woman is a greater witness. After all, the world would see that God is alive and cares enough about His people to come to their rescue. However, the lost world, especially in America is often skeptical of faith healing. They have seen and heard too many stories that just don't add up. Others believe that even if God possessed the power to heal, He would not necessarily heal them. The unbelievers want to know if God loves them enough to intervene, but even more, they want to know if Christ can make a difference in their lives. They want to see proof through the difference Jesus makes in the believer's life. God knows the wisest thing to do in all our circumstances. The Psalmist's goal was not to be blessed for his own happiness, but so that he could be a testimony to others.

Years ago I was sitting in my recliner watching a ball game. One of my small children came in, jumped in my lap and gave me a great big hug and kiss. I thought to myself, "What is this about?" All my children were affectionate, but this was out of the blue. I asked, "What's up?" The reply was, "I just wanted to give you a hug and a kiss." "Why?" was my stupid response. "Just because," was the reply. I think that's a good picture of God—He wants to bless us *just because*. He loves us, just because. He wants to answer our prayers, just because.

God also wants us to love others so much that we see beyond ourselves and become a blessing to them. The only way we can share His love is to experience it ourselves and as we spend time with God in prayer, we begin to sense His love for others.

No other situation illustrates this better than sharing our faith. A few years ago I had the privilege of taking a mission trip to Romania. As I departed from Orlando, I could only think how tired I was. We had just completed a stewardship program for our building campaign. It was one of the most exhausting experiences of my ministry.

After a nine hour flight, we had a layover in Paris. The Paris airport is probably the most difficult airport I have had the pleasure to negotiate. We had to travel in a small bus to get taxied from one gate to the next (which took so long we missed our connector flight). A few stops into our journey, a young lady boarded the bus crying and emotionally distraught, so distraught in fact, I thought at first she was high on something. Instantly, as a pastor, I felt I needed to find out the problem. After all I was traveling with two of my deacons and they would expect me to do something.

Almost in mid-thought I told the Lord that I was tired, hungry and I just woke up. I felt it was a bit hypocritical of me to minister just because I did not want to look bad in front of my men. By the time I rationalized my feelings, someone was already helping the lady. I felt "off the hook."

As we boarded our connector flight, I began to feel rather guilty. I "dug in my heels" with God, reminding Him of how many hours I spend ministering to people and how tired I was feeling.

Of course, you will never guess who sat in front of me on the plane—the young lady (still crying). I found myself getting upset with God. Couldn't someone else help her? I just needed to sleep. Finally, I compromised with God and said I would pray for her. As I prayed, however, I began to feel God's compassion and love for her. Here was someone who was obviously so troubled that her heart was breaking. Certainly she would be open to the love of God.

As I made a move to speak to her, I noticed she had gone to sleep. I kicked myself all the way to Hungary. I began praying for another opportunity. I would get one last small chance.

We landed in Budapest. We went through customs. Then we finally picked up our bags and went to our taxi. There at the curb waiting was the young lady. I approached her and asked if everything was alright. She related to me that her father had died and she had traveled from America to claim his body. I shared with her who I was and more importantly, who Christ was. There was not enough time to make a detailed gospel presentation, and I will forever regret my stubbornness and selfish attitude. I had missed a golden opportunity.

I share this with you not to admit my failures, but to reveal to you that I learned a valuable lesson. **When we allow God's face to shine upon us, we feel His heart, and become His hands.** I often hear people say that people "don't care how much you know until they know how much you care." Or, that others will not listen until they know you love them. I don't think they are interested in how much we love them as much as how much God loves them. I did not love this young lady enough, but God did. I felt that love that day and I believe she did too.

There is a second result of this prayer. Verses 3 and 4 say, *"Let the peoples praise You, O God; Let all the peoples praise You. Let the nations be glad and sing for joy; for You will judge the peoples with uprightness and guide the nations on the earth."* When God blesses us and the way of salvation is known, He is glorified. When people receive Christ, they become worshippers of God. The cross of Christ has been applied to their lives—the blood of Christ has not been wasted on them. God is honored; He is glorified. Verse 4 speaks of God's rulership. When people are led to Christ, He becomes their Lord and God's rulership or Lordship is alive in them.

The final result is that people will fear God. Psalm 67:6, 7 says, *"The earth has yielded its produce; God, our God, blesses us. God blesses us, that all the ends of the earth may fear Him."* They see God in His majesty and power, and have fear in their hearts as they are convicted of their sin. Conviction will lead many to repentance in Christ.

Answers to prayer can lead not only to success but also to significance by making a difference in the lives of others. In the movie "Pearl Harbor," the main character is a pilot who volunteers to go to England to help Europe fight the forces of Hitler. When he arrives things were not as he imagined. The planes were shot up, they were short on pilots and pilots were being killed daily. The soldier who greeted him, knowing he'd volunteered for this duty, asked, "Are you crazy?" "No sir," he replied "I just want to make a difference." That, I believe, needs to be the goal of every believer—pray to get answers in our lives and in the lives of those around us.

I challenge you to begin to pray with confidence in the Lord, committed to the will of God, with a clean heart, with great passion and never giving up on your prayers. Begin today and get the *yes* answers from God.

A CALL TO PRAYER AND FASTING

A Call to Prayer and Fasting

What if I shared a plan with you and if you followed this plan it would draw you closer to God than ever before? What if it would help you overcome bad habits and emotional strongholds? What if the plan would lead you to more answered prayer than you have ever experienced? Would you be interested?

I am referring to a time of prayer and fasting. Fasting is a voluntary and deliberate abstinence from food for the purpose of seeking God through concentrated prayer. Fasting has been practiced in Scripture and throughout history when people were desperate for God to intervene in their lives.

These are desperate times in our world. Desperate times call for desperate measures. You may be going through financially tough times, or perhaps a relationship is in trouble, or you have health issues. You have cried out to God and persevered in prayer but you still find God is silent.

At one time I found myself in desperate times on several fronts. My wife had been diagnosed with breast cancer. She was facing several surgeries and many months of recovery time. The financial crunch at church was quickly becoming a financial crisis. The recession was hitting Central Florida hard. Our church was also adjusting to the termination of a long-tenured staff member and all the difficulties involved in that process. During this period God moved my heart to have a time of prayer and fasting. During that 21-day fast I felt more closely drawn to God than I had in years and I also received some major answers to prayer.

I know you may be tempted to put this book aside because it's hard to think about giving up food for an extended period of time. You think, "I get hungry. I get headaches." You may think, "After all, God gave us food to eat, so just eat it!" I understand your reluctance.

I am reminded of a story about a pastor who visits an elderly lady in her home. His hostess asks him, "Can I get you a cup of coffee or a soft drink?" "I wouldn't mind a Coke," he replies. The lady goes into the kitchen to get his drink. While she is gone, he notices some peanuts on the coffee table. He is famished. He reaches over and takes a handful of nuts and wolfs them down. Just then the lady walks back into the room with a strange look on her face. The pastor, embarrassed, apologizes, "I was just so hungry...I thought you wouldn't mind." She smiles back and replies, "Oh, it's okay. Since I lost my teeth I can't eat them anyway. I just suck off the chocolate and put them back in the bowl."

I know you are thinking, "I can't believe you told that." Well, you lost your appetite, didn't you?

There are over 75 scriptural references to fasting. Daniel fasted for 21 days; David for seven; Esther for three and Jesus fasted for 40 days in the wilderness.

Jesus said in Mark 2:19 and 20, "*While the bridegroom is with them, the attendants of the bridegroom cannot fast, can they? So long as they have the bridegroom with them, they cannot fast. But the days will come when the bridegroom is taken away from them, and then they will fast in that day."* Although Jesus never commanded us to fast, He did encourage it. Fasting began in Jewish culture as people mourned the death of a loved one. Their grief was so great they would not eat. Later it became a way to humble themselves before God out of desperation. Then it became a spiritual exercise. For example, the Jews were commanded to fast on the Day of Atonement. Eventually fasting became synonymous with humbling yourself before God for a special season of prayer. So, why fast today? Why abstain from food that God has provided? How do we fast and for how long?

Isaiah 58 is one of the most comprehensive passages on fasting. Ironically, God is rebuking the people for fasting in the wrong way and for the wrong reason. We pick up the story where Isaiah is talking to the people about fasting and praying while they were neglecting ministry.

> "Cry loudly, do not hold back; raise your voice like a trumpet, and declare to My people their transgression and to the house of Jacob their sins. Yet they seek Me day by day and delight to know My ways, as a nation that has done righteousness and has not forsaken the ordinance of their God they ask Me for just decisions, they delight in the nearness of God. 'Why have we fasted and You do not see? Why have we humbled ourselves and You do not notice?' Behold, on the day of your fast you find your desire, and drive hard all your workers. Behold, you fast for contention and strife and to strike with a wicked fist you do not fast

like you do today to make your voice heard on high. Is it a fast like this which I choose, a day for a man to humble himself? Is it for bowing one's head like a reed and for spreading out sackcloth and ashes as a bed? Will you call this a fast, even an acceptable day to the LORD?" (Isaiah 58:1-5)

Then after the first five verses, he begins to outline for us the benefits and purposes of fasting.

"Is this not the fast which I choose, to loosen the bonds of wickedness, to undo the bands of the yoke, and to let the oppressed go free and break every yoke? Is it not to divide your bread with the hungry and bring the homeless poor into the house; when you see the naked, to cover him; and not to hide yourself from your own flesh? Then your light will break out like the dawn, and your recovery will speedily spring forth; and your righteousness will go before you; the glory of the LORD will be your rear guard. Then you will call, and the LORD will answer; you will cry, and He will say, 'Here I am ' if you remove the yoke from your midst, the pointing of the finger and speaking wickedness, and if you give yourself to the hungry and satisfy the desire of the afflicted, then your light will rise in darkness and your gloom will become like midday. And the LORD will continually guide you, and satisfy your desire in scorched places, and give strength to your bones; and you will be like a watered garden, and like a spring of water whose waters do not fail. Those from among you will rebuild the ancient ruins; you will raise up the age-old foundations; and you will be called the repairer of the breach, the restorer of the streets in which to dwell." (Isaiah 58:6-12)

THE PURPOSES OF FASTING

As we look at the purposes of fasting, we find the first reason in verse 6. *"Is this not the fast which I choose, to loosen the bonds of wickedness..."* Let's call this a freedom from spiritual bondage. When we think about bondage, we usually think of a non-believer receiving Christ and being set free from sin. However, Christians can be under bondage as well. In II Corinthians 10:4 and 5, Paul calls them fortresses or strongholds.

> "... for the weapons of our warfare are not of the flesh, but divinely powerful for the destruction of fortresses. We are destroying speculations and every lofty thing raised up against the knowledge of God, and we are taking every thought captive to the obedience of Christ..."

These strongholds often begin with a thought. Satan places a sinful thought in our minds and we accept it as truth; then we act upon it. If we do not genuinely repent, a toehold (or a beachhead) is formed in our life. A habit begins to develop. If unchecked, this toehold turns into a foothold and then Satan has a stronghold in our lives. This sinful habit is accepted as part of our life as we justify its existence. Yet, this stronghold is quietly tearing away at our spiritual life.

When we fast, God speaks loudly in our lives. As we are driven to prayer we also develop a clearer picture of how God sees us. We see things from God's perspective instead of our own rationalization when God applies the truth of His Word to our hearts.

When my nephew started the first grade he got into trouble for talking the very first day. The second day, his mom asked him if he got into trouble again. He replied, "Well, a little bit." His mom asked, "What's a little bit?" He said, "I was in a straight line, but everybody else wasn't." We all have a tendency to see things from our own perspective but when we fast, we have an opportunity to better see God's perspective.

God hates our sin and we need to hate it too. When we hate the sin we will no longer want it as part of our life; this leads us to repentance. Deep repentance is the only avenue to release strongholds in our lives.

The second reason we need to fast is because we have heavy burdens in our lives. Isaiah 58, verse 6 goes on to read, "...*loosen the bonds of wickedness, to undo the bands of the yoke...*" or more simply put—to release our burdens.

Perhaps as you read this you are battling health issues, relationship problems or financial burdens. It's like you have a 500 pound weight on your chest and every week someone is coming along and adding another 50 pounds to the load. You think, "I just can't take it anymore."

Only the Lord can lift these burdens. Jesus said, *"Come to Me, all who are weary and heavy-laden, and I will give you rest. Take My yoke upon you and learn from Me, for I am gentle and humble in heart, and YOU WILL FIND REST FOR YOUR SOULS. For My yoke is easy and My burden is light." (Matthew 11:28-30)* Whenever you spend concentrated time with God, He will lift burdens and comfort you. Fasting gives you that avenue of concentration.

A third purpose is to bring about the outpouring of God's Spirit. Isaiah 58:6 continues, *"...and to let the oppressed go free..."* Perhaps it may seem that I am stretching things a bit as the Spirit is not mentioned. However, this is slavery imagery. One of the sins of Israel's day that this chapter addresses was the oppression the people were under. The leaders would fast but they would not help the poor or minister to those in need. Fasting had no real affect on their lives. They were in need of personal revival.

As I look at our nation and communities, I am amazed at the changes that have taken place over the past decade. Knowledge and technology is doubling in capacity every few years. Children are growing up faster in knowledge and slower in maturity. When I began in ministry most of the people I shared Christ with were already knowledgeable of the gospel. On a 1-to-10 scale (10 being ready to receive Christ), I would say the average person was sitting at 7 or 8. I think today's average is closer to 2 or 3. Atheism is growing in America and indifference to the things of God is at epidemic proportion. We need an outpouring of God's Spirit.

The only century when America did not experience a great sweeping revival was the 20th Century. The First Great Awakening (18th Century) began in a time of prayer and fasting. The Second Great Awakening (19th Century) began with prayer and fasting. What about us?

God's Spirit is certainly being poured out in other parts of the world. Christianity in India has grown from 1% to 10% over the past 10 years.[1] God is at work in China. 47% of the people of Africa are Christian believers.[2] What about here? The Holy Spirit decides where the winds of revival will blow next. *"The wind blows where it wishes and you hear the sound of it, but do not know where it comes from and where it is going; so is everyone who is born of the Spirit."* *(John 3:8)* We can fast, pray and ask God to bring revival to our nation and our towns. In the Old Testament we read, *"… and My people who are called by My name humble themselves and pray and seek My face and turn from their wicked ways, then I will*

hear from heaven, will forgive their sin and will heal their land."
(II Chronicles 7:14) Fasting became synonymous with humility in
New Testament times, so we need to humble ourselves and pray.

THE NEXT GREAT REVIVAL
COULD BEGIN WITH YOU!

Isaiah 58:6 also gives us our fourth purpose for fasting—a freedom
from emotional burdens. This yoke is not just about strongholds of
sinful habits in our lives, but emotional strongholds as well. While
one may have an emotional stronghold of anger or bitterness, others may experience a stronghold of depression.

The good news is that we do not have to live this way. In 1
Kings 18, Elijah challenged and battled 450 prophets of Baal. After
scoring a great victory for God, Elijah's life was threatened by the
wicked Queen Jezebel. Emotionally drained, he ran and the next
scene finds him crying to God for death, but God restored Elijah
after a time of prayer and fasting.

Isaiah 58:7 teaches *"Is it not to divide your bread with the hun-*
gry and bring the homeless poor into the house; when you see the
naked, to cover him; and not to hide yourself from your own flesh?"
We read here what was happening in Isaiah's day. People were
hungry all around them. Basically God's question is, "Look, when
you fast, doesn't it remind you of all the hunger that surrounds
you? When your stomach churns, don't you know there are people
in the world who experience starvation everyday?" Sometimes we
get so caught up in our own lives that we fail to notice the needs of
others around us. Fasting helps us to see that the world does not
revolve around us. In meeting the needs of others, we are not giving in to our emotions about ourselves.

Still another reason for fasting is found in verse 8. *"Then your light will break through the dawn."* Light is often a symbol in Scripture of knowledge or understanding. It is said we are a product of the decisions we have made. If this is true, then getting God's guidance and direction in making those decisions is vital. No one but God can see the future and He is not often motivated to share His grand blueprint with us. However, I have found that when I fast, God seems to speak louder. I can sense His guidance, direction and connection in my life in a clearer way.

In Acts 13 a decision was made that changed the world. Before the ascension, Jesus told His disciples to take the gospel to the uttermost parts of the earth. By the end of the first 12 chapters of Acts, the gospel had still not spread beyond Jerusalem. Acts 12 speaks of the persecution that broke out against Christians. What were the disciples to do? In Acts 13 it says, *"Now there were at Antioch, in the church that was there, prophets and teachers: Barnabas, and Simeon who was called Niger, and Lucius of Cyrene, and Manaen who had been brought up with Herod the tetrarch, and Saul. While they were ministering to the Lord and fasting, the Holy Spirit said, "Set apart for Me Barnabas and Saul for the work to which I have called them." Then, when they had fasted and prayed and laid their hands on them, they sent them away."*

Here we find a small group of people fasting and praying. From that prayer meeting, Paul and Barnabas were sent out as the first missionaries. A few centuries later Christianity would become the predominant religion in the Roman Empire. **Today the gospel message is spread throughout every part of the world and it all began with five people meeting for an intense time of prayer and fasting.**

THE PRACTICE OF FASTING

How do you fast? Do you stop eating all food; stop all solid foods; just sodas? What's the correct way to fast? The Bible presents some options but much depends on your reason for fasting. If it's for spiritual reasons, which I am advocating, you have a few choices. Some people fast on liquids only, such as water and juices. Although some may frown upon this, your goal is not discipline, but concentrated prayer. If you take a small amount of juice from time to time, it will help your energy level and help you to prolong your fast. I know there are others who fast by omitting a certain item from their diet. This can be bread, soft drinks, sweets, etc. This is often symbolic of sacrifice on their part as they seek the Lord to bless a certain ministry. While this is a good practice, it will not necessarily bring the results I am speaking about in this chapter.

The length of a fast can be very important. I have fasted for various periods of time, but one particular 21-day fast was by far the best for me. I worked through the spiritual cobwebs of my life in the first three or four days. Let me say this very clearly, if you are not going to pray and spend time with God, there is no need to fast—it's a waste of time. It's the prayer that makes a difference, not the abstinence from food. It's not about twisting God's arm or trying to impress Him. Fasting is all about prayer.

THE PROMISES OF FASTING

So what are the benefits? As we have learned from Isaiah 58:8, the will of God becomes clearer and we will experience new strength. God will reveal His power in our lives and we will also receive answers to prayer. During my 21-day fast, I laid certain requests before the Lord. It was these burdens that originally drove me to fast.

The first burden on my heart was for my wife, the year she was diagnosed with breast cancer. Because of her family history, we felt that a double mastectomy was needed. Our major concern was whether the cancer had spread to the lymph nodes and thereby, potentially to her entire body. After her surgery, the lymph nodes were sent for testing and the results came back negative. Today by the grace of God, Pam is cancer free!

Another prayer burden was the finances of our church when we moved into a new 2,700 seat Worship Center. A few months later the recession hit. Man, did it hit! Central Florida seemed to be especially hurt. In the midst of all the economic woes, we were committed to conduct back-to-back capital campaigns to raise funds for the building. Time for the second campaign was approaching and we needed the money to make the payment on the building. I fasted and prayed that God would make the campaign positive and not negative in difficult financial times.

On the fourth day of the fast, God clearly directed me to do two things: postpone the campaign until fall and share the financial state of the church with the congregation. The Sunday that I shared this direction with the church, the postponement was looked upon as wise and the church offerings increased enough to provide for the building until the fall campaign. All of this seemed to lift a burden and draw our people together.

A third prayer concerned general church unity following the dismissal of a long-tenured staff member. Although there was no immorality involved, the Personnel Committee and I felt we faced little choice but his termination. This caused a ripple of disunity within the church body. People loyal to this employee left the church and there was further collateral damage as other loyalties were tested. We needed God to do something to draw us back to our purpose and vision. Judgement House™—our alternative to Halloween—with its great evangelistic success was God's *yes* answer. Throughout this ministry event our members were united with an unusual joy. More than 500 of our members were involved in making this event a huge success because over 550 of the 8,000 people who attended came to know Christ. God used Judgement House™ to bring our members together in service and to remind us once again of why we exist as a church—to reach people for Jesus Christ.

A fourth answer to prayer came as I was praying for a ministerial staff position to be filled. On the last day of my fast, I received a call from our candidate. He informed me that he was 100% sure that God was leading him to our church. Although this move did not work out long-term, the man had a meaningful ministry while he was here and God also gave our church an opportunity to minister to him in his time of real need.

There were many other specific answers, but perhaps the greatest blessing was to see glimpses of revival in our church.

Isaiah 58:11, 12 teaches us, *"And the LORD will continually guide you, and satisfy your desire in scorched places, and give strength to your bones; and you will be like a watered garden, and like a spring of water whose waters do not fail. Those from among you will rebuild the ancient ruins; You will raise up the age-old foundations; and you will be called the repairer of the breach, the restorer of the streets in which to dwell."*

These verses teach that God will restore what once was lost. Perhaps you feel you lost something with God that you want restored. Maybe you made some bad decisions and you would like at least some of those consequences removed. I believe as you fast and pray He will bring restoration.

WHAT TO DO

Let me encourage you to begin a fast. You could start with a 24-hour fast—6:00 p.m. to 6:00 p.m. Make your prayer list, spend the day in prayer, then allow God to enter deep into your heart and soul to change your life.

For those who have experience in fasting, I encourage you to expand and challenge yourself—fast from solid food for a week or even longer. God will do a special work in your life. Let's give God an opportunity to say *yes* in your life.

GETTING STARTED

APPENDIX II

GETTING STARTED

I have heard that 90 percent of rocket fuel is used at the launching pad. Getting started is often challenging as we try to launch new habits in our lives. Earlier I mentioned that I use a tool called "The Spiritual Journal" to help me in my devotional and prayer time with God. I have included a weekly prayer journal in this appendix to help you get started.

The process begins with daily prayer requests. These are people or situations that I want to pray about every day. I place the person's name in the left hand column; the request in the middle column; and then in the right hand column, the date the request was answered.

I usually divide up the days of the week. For example, on Monday I pray for my church staff (I am a pastor). On Tuesday I pray for our deacons, other family members, government and military. On Wednesday I pray for the requests of the church. On Thursday I pray for my fellow pastors across the country. On Friday I pray for the missionaries, many of whom send me requests. On Saturday I pray for the unbelievers in our area, specifically for the ones I know. Finally on Sunday, I pray for our church services and our Small Group Bible Fellowship teachers.

I hope this guide helps. You are welcome to duplicate these prayer sheets; however, I do encourage you to make an investment in some type of journal. If not "The Spiritual Journal," then a tool similar to keep you committed.

We used these spiritual journals when I led our entire church through a video series of Bible studies entitled "Discovering Spiritual Maturity." For more information about this video series, please log onto our website at

www.WinningEdgeTV.org or
www.fbcoviedo.org

Or call our church office at 407-365-3484.

I leave you with one final verse…

> but just as it is written, "THINGS WHICH EYE HAS NOT SEEN AND EAR HAS NOT HEARD, AND which HAVE NOT ENTERED THE HEART OF MAN, ALL THAT GOD HAS PREPARED FOR THOSE WHO LOVE HIM." (I Corinthians 2:9)

SAMPLE

Name	Prayer Request	Date Answered
John	For employment	1-17-09
	Sister's cancer	
Bob	Healing for cancer	2-2-09
Pam	Speaking opportunity in Jax	2-13-09
Tom B.	Salvation—opportunity to share Christ with Him	2-9-09

MONDAY

Name	Prayer Request	Date Answered

TUESDAY

Name	Prayer Request	Date Answered

WEDNESDAY

Name	Prayer Request	Date Answered

THURSDAY

Name	Prayer Request	Date Answered

FRIDAY

Name	Prayer Request	Date Answered

SATURDAY

Name	Prayer Request	Date Answered

SUNDAY

Name	Prayer Request	Date Answered

ENDNOTES

Introduction

[1] World Catalog (worldcat.org) provided by Southeastern Baptist Theological Seminary Library, Wake Forest, North Carolina, n.d.

[2] James Merritt, "How to Connect with God" (Snellville, Georgia, n.d.), p. 1. from "Talking to God" Newsweek, (January 6, 1992).

[3] Ravi Zacharias, Has Christianity Failed You? (Grand Rapids, Michigan, Zondervan, 2010), 143, 144.

Chapter 1

[1] Samuel J. Schultz, The Old Testament Speaks, (New York, New York, Harper and Row, 1970) 199.

[2] Dr. Gerald McGraw, Old Testament Class, (Toccoa Falls College, Toccoa, Georgia, Fall 1977).

[3] Dick Eastman, No Easy Road, (Grand Rapids, Michigan, Baker Book House, 1971),115.

[4] Charles Stanley, Sermon on Prayer, "The Chapel Hour" television broadcast, (Atlanta, Georgia, n.d.)

[5] R. A. Torrey, How to Pray, (Old Tappan, New Jersey, Spire Books, 1975), 24.

[6] James Dobson, Focus on the Family radio broadcast, (Colorado Springs, Colorado, n.d.).

[7] Larry Dawsey, "Does Prayer Heal?" Readers Digest, Volume 148, Number 887 (March 1996), 116-119.

Chapter 2

[1]James Merritt sermon, "Going to the Head of the Class," (Snellville, Georgia, May 20, 2003), 7, sermon search.com.

[2] Louis Hodges, Toccoa Falls College, lecture (Toccoa, Georgia 1977).

[3]S.M. Lockridge, Sermon 1976, San Diego, California, Internet site "Captive Heart" March 26, 2007.

[4]Sermon Central Pro, Internet site, Sermoncentral.com. Remarks made by Ted Turner in Orlando, Florida, 1990, American Humanist Association

Chapter 3

[1]John Maxwell, Lecture, (Orlando, Florida, n.d).

[2]Henry T. Blackaby and Claude V. King, Experiencing God: Knowing and Doing the Will of God, (Nashville, Tennessee, Lifeway Press, 1990), 73.

[3]Ray Stedman, sermon "Praying Boldly," (Palo Alto, California, Discovery Publication, 1995), 3.
[4] Ibid

Chapter 4

[1]John Lavender, Why Prayers Are Unanswered, Sermon Central. com, n.d.

[2]Charles Stanley, Forgiveness, (Nashville, Tennessee, Oliver Nelson, 1987), 16.

[3]The Barna Group, "Born Again Christians Just as likely to Divorce as are Non-Christians," September 8, 2004.

[4]Sharon Jayson, "Women Rule the Roost and that's OK with Men," USA Today.com.

[5]Ibid

[6]Ibid

[7]Theodore Baldick, lecture at Mid America Theological Seminary, (Memphis, Tennessee, January 10, 1990).

[8]Ibid

[9]Ibid

Chapter 5

[1]"It's a Wonderful Life," movie, January 7, 1947 written by Francis Goodrich

[2]Bill Gothard, The Power of Crying Out, (Colorado Springs, Colorado, Multnomah Publishers, 2002), 74.

[3]Bill Gothard, The Power of Crying Out, (Colorado Springs, Colorado, Multnomah Publishers, 2002), 26.

[4]Bill Gothard, The Power of Crying Out, (Colorado Springs, Colorado, Multnomah Publishers, 2002), 14.

Chapter 6

[1]James Dobson

[2]Ravi Zacharias, Cries of the Heart, (Nashville, Tennessee, Word Press, 1998), 40.

Chapter 7

[1]John Maxwell, "The Difference Between Success and Significance," (Injoy, Atlanta, Georgia, Mission Impact Volume 5, Number 6, n.d.), 1

[2]Rusty Rustenbach, "Giving Yourself Away", Ibid, 2.

[3]C. F. Keil and F. Delitzsch, <u>Volume 5 Psalms</u>, (Peabody, Massachusetts, Hendrickson Publishers, original publishing date 1866, this publication—2006), p. 440.

Appendix I

[1]Conversation with Larry Reesor, President of Global Focus, January 20, 2011, Orlando FL.

[2]Ibid